DELECTABLE DESSERTS

Delicious Connections volume 1

Marina Michaels

Athena Star
PRESS

A note from the author. Understanding the hard work that goes into making any kind of book, and especially a cookbook, and knowing the possibilities for error on the path to publication even despite recipe testing and editing, I can appreciate how errors creep in. I fervently hope I haven't introduced any. If I have, it would be a great favor to me if you were to let me know. You can contact me by writing me care of the publisher, or emailing me at marina@sonic.net. Thank you!

Athena Star Press
2467 Westvale Court
Santa Rosa, California 95403
athenastarpress.com

Print ISBN 978-1-60038-007-5

eBook ISBN 978-1-60038-020-4

Printed in the United States of America with chlorine-free ink and on acid-free interior paper stock supplied by a Forest Stewardship Council-certified provider.

First Edition May 2019

Third printing

Contents

Custards, Mousses, and Ice Cream 87

Frostings and Sweet Sauces 103

Introduction

ood connects us. It's essential to life, but it doesn't have to be boring. So we humans have come up with an awe-inspiring variety of ways to prepare foods, both savory and sweet. And we all love to share our food. Every culture—and family—has favorites, and we share those favorites with our brothers and sisters around the planet, on occasions large and small, for important reasons or no reason except the joy of sharing.

When someone shares a recipe with us, we often change the recipe to suit ourselves—a little more *this*, a little less *that*, and now we have our own version. There isn't just *one* Mardi Gras King Cake recipe—there are dozens, each with a story and a connection between the people who shared those recipes and the people who modified them.

When I make a recipe someone shared with me, or that was handed down by my mother (who got it from her mother, who got it from *her* mother), I think of the person who shared the recipe. I like to imagine other people in different places and times enjoying the recipe and making it their own, so that we have an endlessly creative proliferation of versions of cultural favorites. And sometimes when making a recipe, I remember people who are now gone, but whose love is still with me through the recipes they shared.

This book is my curated collection of favorite dessert recipes, gathered over decades, starting when I was in my early teens. These are the best of the best: recipes I make over and over again because they are consistently delicious.

Some are originals, invented by family, friends, or me. Some are my version of a classic that you may have in your collection. As with all classics, my versions have my own special touches. A few recipes have been handed down through generations of my family. Some of these recipes were popular long ago; they're still excellent. If you don't already have your own version, perhaps they'll be a delightful discovery for you and yours.

In the headnotes for each recipe, I share notes and stories: sometimes a memory of the person who shared the recipe, sometimes tidbits about the recipe's history, sometimes just a note about how much my family enjoys the recipe, or some serving suggestions. To me, those stories are important parts of the recipe because they connect us to people in other places and times. I hope they help you feel the connections to others that recipes can foster..

Your Level of Baking Expertise

My mother always baked from scratch, and that's how I bake too. I wrote all instructions so they are clear and unambiguous, and most of these recipes are easy to make. If you know the baking basics (how to measure—or weigh—and mix ingredients, how to use a range and oven, and how to judge when something is done), you'll be fine. If you're an absolute beginner, you might need to look up a few terms or techniques. If you follow the instructions carefully, the recipes should work every time.

If a recipe doesn't work, carefully check that you included all ingredients and didn't skip a step. And be comforted in knowing that even the most experienced baker has the occasional failure—just ask any cook! We commiserate, sometimes have a good laugh, then move on. In baking, as in life, everything is a learning experience.

Finding Recipes in This Book

To make it easy for you to find recipes,

- The chapters, and the recipes in each chapter, are in alphabetical order.
- Each recipe is in the table of contents.
- I simplified most recipe names so that they are logical and straightforward. In some cases, the name was charming enough or well-known enough (or was named by or after the recipe's originator) that I kept it.
- In addition, to help you find recipes to suit your needs, some common main ingredients of each recipe are indexed. For example, you can look up *egg whites* in the index to find all recipes that use egg whites. (Very handy when you have leftover egg whites or yolks.)

Ingredient Guidelines
•••

As is true for any cooking adventure, it's a good idea to read each recipe all the way through to make sure you know what you need and what's involved.

The ingredients within each recipe are listed in the order in which you'll use them in the recipe. Each step in a recipe's instructions is one action. For example, if you are to combine two ingredients, that's one step..

This commonsense approach makes it easier for you to stay on track with the recipe. If you find that the instructions call for an ingredient listed after an ingredient you don't recall using, double-check the previous steps of the recipe to see if you missed a step. A helpful cooking practice is to lay the ingredients out on the counter in the order in which you will be using them. (I put each ingredient away after I use it, but that's possibly too efficient.)

In recipes where an ingredient is used for two or more parts of a recipe, I list the ingredient once but give the individual measurements. For example, a recipe might call for 1 cup plus 1 tablespoon cocoa. The cup is used in one part of the recipe, and the tablespoon in another. That way, you know up front how much you need.

For the best flavors, use the best ingredients you can afford, and use organic ingredients and eggs from pasture-raised chickens when possible. Also, pro tip: fats absorb flavors more readily than other ingredients, so for many of my recipes, I add the vanilla extract (or other flavorings) to the butter first.

Chocolate and Cocoa Powder Guidelines

I love chocolate, so you'll find a disproportionate number of recipes using chocolate and cocoa powder in this book. I make no apologies.

I'm sure by now everyone knows chocolate has ancient origins; anthropologists have found traces of chocolate in Olmec drinking cups dating to 1900 BCE. (The Olmec are the earliest known major Mesoamerican civilization; they thrived in what is now south-central Mexico.)

Chocolate and cocoa powder both come from the cacao tree's seeds (the seeds are called beans). In the following discussion, I've greatly simplified the processes by which we arrive at chocolate and cocoa powder, giving you the essentials any baker needs to know. If you're interested in finding out more about chocolate and cocoa powder, you can find a lot more information online or in books

Once chocolate came to Europe in the 1500s, it became hugely popular, to the point of causing trouble in the Catholic church. Was it okay to drink during mass? While fasting? Some of the dispute was over whether chocolate was a liquid or a solid. The issue was resolved in 1662 when Pope Alexander VII declared that *Liquidum non frangit jejunum* (liquids don't violate the fast). This declaration covered chocolate and coffee, both of which were thought to be medicinal.

Types of Chocolate

Chocolate is a hard substance made from cacao beans. Chocolate, which naturally contains a fat called cocoa butter, is quite bitter. It's made into baking chocolate (unsweetened and sweetened) for use in baking and cooking. Baking chocolate is usually sold in bars or squares, though it comes in other forms as well.

Unsweetened chocolate is just that—ground cacao beans without added sugar. Sweetened chocolates comes in two types: milk and dark.

- **Milk chocolate** has milk and sugar added and doesn't have a lot of chocolate.
- **Dark chocolate** has additional fat and sugar and chocolate. Dark chocolate divides into semisweet and bittersweet chocolates, which are usually interchangeable in a recipe. Baking chocolate and chocolate chip packages declare a percentage of cacao—that percentage is how much of the cacao bean is still in there.

There's also a substance called **white chocolate**, which is made from cocoa butter with the chocolate (cocoa solids) removed and milk added. Many people (and countries) don't recognize this as chocolate, though it has its place in the baking world.

Types of Cocoa Powder

Cocoa powder is a powder made after all the cocoa butter is extracted from cacao beans, which are then ground to a fine powder. Cocoa powder comes in two forms: natural and Dutch process. The two types of cocoa taste different.

- **Natural cocoa powder** is exactly what it sounds like—ground cacao beans with nothing further done to them. (Remember, I'm simplifying here.) Natural cocoa is a bit acidic and usually a lighter brown than its Dutch process cousin.
- **Dutch process cocoa powder** has been treated to neutralize cocoa's natural acidity and make it less bitter. Dutch process cocoa is a richer, deeper brown than natural cocoa. My favorite Dutch process cocoa is Valrhona, which you can get at ChocoSphere.com.

For many recipes, you can use either type of cocoa depending on which you prefer, with one exception: because baking is chemistry, the acidity of the cocoa powder is important in recipes that use baking soda or baking powder for leavening, such as cakes.

- If a recipe uses **baking soda** for leavening, use natural cocoa powder, which is acidic.
- If a recipe uses **baking powder** for leavening, use the more neutral Dutch process cocoa powder.
- If the recipe calls for **an acidic ingredient**, such as sour cream or buttermilk, you can usually use either type of cocoa.
- If a recipe calls for **both baking soda and baking powder,** or if a recipe doesn't use leavening (such as frostings or puddings), you can use either type of cocoa.

Bakers are becoming more savvy, so modern versions of classic recipes often specify which type of cocoa powder to use. I've updated my recipes accordingly. If one of the recipes in this book doesn't state which type of cocoa to use, you can use either.

This use of baking soda versus baking powder is true for other ingredients; for example, if a recipe calls for buttermilk, which is slightly acidic, you'll notice the leavening is baking soda. Buttermilk, by the way, is a wonderful addition to cakes (and pancakes!)—it makes them light and tender.

Types of Sugars

Sugar comes in a remarkable number of forms. All the most commonly used forms of sugar are variations on the theme of granulated sugar, which is a fine sugar made from sugar canes or beets. Older recipes often refer to granulated sugar as white sugar or even just sugar—it was understood that this meant granulated sugar. Other common types of sugar are

- **Brown sugar** (called red sugar once upon a long time ago), which is refined granulated sugar with molasses. Often, recipes specify light or dark brown sugar. In the United Kingdom (UK), light brown sugar is called demerara, though in the US demerara is a specific type of brown sugar, and dark brown sugar is called dark soft sugar—an apt description.) I've found that most recipes work fine using either light or dark brown sugar, so I don't usually specify which in these recipes—use whichever you prefer. In fact, you can sometimes even use brown sugar instead of granulated sugar, though the flavor will be richer and more robust. The main thing to know is that when measuring brown sugar, you usually need to pack it firmly into the measuring cup (the sugar holds the cup shape when dumped out).
- **Powdered sugar,** sometimes also called confectioner's sugar. (What we call it in the US seems to be a regional thing, like whether we call a carbonated beverage soda or pop or even generically "coke" to mean any carbonated

beverage.) In Great Britain and Canada, powdered sugar is called icing sugar. Powdered sugar is granulated sugar ground to a very fine powder. It almost always contains cornstarch, though most organic powdered sugars use tapioca starch instead. If you need to avoid corn, buy organic powdered sugar and make sure the package says it's free of cornstarch.

- **Superfine (castor/caster) sugar**—finely ground granulated sugar. If you need superfine sugar and can't find it in your local market, you can make your own by whirring up regular granulated sugar in a strong blender or spice grinder.

I admire how ingenious we humans are in creating variety out of what seems like a simple foodstuff.

Gluten Free? Paleo? Vegan? Vegetarian?

My daughter is healthier when eating gluten free, so over the years I've worked at either converting favorite recipes to gluten-free versions, or finding good gluten-free recipes. Most of my experiments have been with America's Test Kitchen's (ATK) gluten-free flour mix. Because I don't want to ask you to make your own ATK gluten-free flour (it's a bit fussy), I haven't included any gluten-free recipes that use ATK's flour blend. ATK's *The How Can It Be Gluten Free Cookbook* (America's Test Kitchen, 2014) has many excellent recipes, all of which work. I highly recommend it.

However, this cookbook does include a number of gluten-free recipes, including the Chocolate Decadence Cake (page 21), the scrumptious Almond Crescents (page 65), and the super-simple Peanut Butter Cookies (page 81).

The paleo diet and the kinds of desserts in this cookbook don't go together. (Though you'll find one paleo-friendly recipe—the Banana Muffins on page 142.)

Only a few recipes are vegan (some of the candy recipes); almost all the recipes are vegetarian for vegetarians who eat dairy and possibly eggs.

Look in the index for other recipes that suit these diets.

Reducing Salt and Sugar Intake

We've all heard how important it is to reduce the salt and sugar in our diets. I've found that salt is not essential to the flavor (or chemistry) of many recipes, so I've removed it from those recipes. Therefore, the majority of these recipes contain no added salt (or just a tiny bit), and generally use unsalted butter. In some cases, a recipe calls for salt because the results will taste flat without it. When a recipe calls for salt, I use Himalayan pink salt. Regular salt is fine.

Many people are concerned about sugar. I believe that sugar in intelligent moderation is fine. I've included a few recipes with little or no refined sugar. If you want or need to avoid sugar completely, I encourage you to check out the many specialty dessert cookbooks that focus on low- and no-sugar recipes.

About Using Butter

Since the 1990s, we've been told to avoid trans fats (found in partially hy-drogenated oils such as shortening and margarine), though scientists reported the dangers in the 1970s. Over the years, I've adapted my recipes as needed to remove trans fats. For example, if someone shared a recipe that called for margarine or shortening, I tested it with butter.

However, some people are concerned about butter's cholesterol and saturated fats. If you're one of those folks, you can substitute equal amounts of margarine or shortening for the butter in most of these recipes.

Depending on the recipe's chemistry, in addition to margarine or shortening, you can try substituting any of the following for butter. Be aware that in some cases, the recipe won't come out right if you don't use butter, and the flavor will be different.

- Apple sauce (unsweetened). Substitute cup for cup, or use for half the butter; for example, if the recipe calls for one cup butter, you can use one cup applesauce, or you can use a half cup applesauce and a half cup butter.
- Buttermilk, sour cream, or yogurt. (Some people say you can also substitute cream cheese.) Substitute cup for cup.
- Coconut oil. Substitute cup for cup.
- Vegetable oil (a light one, like avocado oil). Use ¾ cup oil for each cup butter.

In these recipes, when you see "butter," that's grade AA unsalted butter (unless otherwise specified). If you only have salted butter, slightly reduce any salt the recipe calls for.

About Flour, and Sifting It

Unless otherwise specified, all the recipes that call for flour are for unbleached, all-purpose flour. I risk horrifying some people, but I stopped sifting flour decades ago and my recipes come out fine; it's just one less step and speeds the baking that much more. Sift if you like, but these recipes don't need it.

However, be aware that aside from a few exceptions, ingredients must be well mixed to come together for baking magic, whether you sift or not.

You should always measure the flour (and all ingredients!) carefully and spoon it into the measuring cup (rather than scooping), but even that's not essential.

Understanding Prep/Cook Times

Each recipe includes a *Prep/cook time*. This time represents how much time you can expect to spend on a recipe from start to finish. Prep/cook time includes all preparation tasks (grating, chopping, measuring, and so on), as well as all mixing, cooking, cooling, and setting-up times.

The prep/cook times are as accurate as I can make them based on my own experiences. However, take them as approximations. Many things can make a difference in the amount of preparation and cooking time required.

Baking by Volume or Weight

Traditionally, American cooks have been all over the place in terms of how they specify the amount of each ingredient. Older recipes (and even some newer ones) might call for a pound of butter, for example. Most often, American recipes called for ingredients by volume, not weight. This practice was popularized by Fannie Farmer's popular (and still in print) *The Boston Cooking-School Cook Book* (Little, Brown & Company, 1896), which introduced to the world the idea using standardized measurements.

More than a century later, cooks all over the world are sharing their recipes (hurray!), recipes whose ingredients are specified either in the same-sounding volume (cups, for example), but whose volumes aren't the same (a measuring cup in America holds less than a measuring cup in the UK), or are specified in metric units (grams, milliliters). Recipes can go wrong, sometimes disastrously wrong, if you use the wrong volume or weight.

In these recipes, I've kept the American volumes (cups, teaspoons, and so on), but for cooks who prefer to cook by weight, or who are in another country, I've included several tables in *Weights and Measures* (page 149) giving the UK and metric equivalents for many common ingredients.

Paired with this American practice of specifying ingredients by volume has been the practice of specifying ingredients by package or unit (one package cream cheese, one stick butter, for example). This practice makes sense—a package is, after all, a type of volume.

But packages have changed in America, so a package of cream cheese is no longer always and reliably eight ounces—it could be five ounces, or three. And sticks of butter vary in volume as well. Plus baking chocolate is now sold in a wider variety of shapes and sizes. One popular baking chocolate bar, which was once sold in packages of one-ounce squares, is now half-ounce squares. If you didn't know that, and you were following a recipe that called for three squares of baking chocolate, your recipe just wouldn't be chocolatey enough, and that's just tragic.

To address the issue of package sizes, I've updated and standardized all recipes so that they call for the volumes or weight of ingredients. For example, for a recipe that called for 1 square chocolate, I've changed that to 1 ounce.

Baking Outside the US

All these recipes should work in any country, though you may need to make a few adjustments.

- **American measuring cups and spoons** are smaller than cups and spoons used in Australia, Canada, and the UK. See Ingredient Weights and Measures on page 154 for tables showing the equivalent capacities. Those tables also include metric weights and volumes.
- The **temperatures** in these recipes are in Fahrenheit. See the next section (*Oven Temperatures*) for the corresponding temperatures in Celsius or gas marks.
- **American butter** isn't the same as European style butter. European style butter has a higher butterfat content, less water, and is a tiny bit sour (because it's cultured). American butter has a lower percentage of butterfat, more water, and a more neutral flavor. The water in American butter helps leaven baked goods. If you substitute European style butter for American style in baked foods, the results will be greasier and drier. To counteract that, if you only have European-style butter, try using about ¾ of the amount of butter called for, and experiment with adding a tiny splash of water. For example, if a recipe calls for 1 cup of butter, try ¾ of a cup European style butter with a teaspoon of water. (European style butter should be fine for frostings as-is.)
- **Egg sizes** can differ, as well as type of eggs (goose, for example, or duck). The eggs used in this cookbook are large, US Grade AA or A chicken eggs. For more information, see Egg Sizes and Substitutions on page 152.

Oven Temperatures

All temperatures are in degrees Fahrenheit (F) in a conventional electric oven. Your oven may cook hotter or cooler than mine.

I almost never preheat the oven, The United States Department of Agriculture says it's not necessary in most cases. When it's important, I've kept that instruction in the recipe. If you don't preheat, and the instructions call for it, you may need to bake the item a little longer. If you do preheat and the instructions don't call for that,shorten your baking times.

If you're used to cooking in Celsius or with a gas mark oven, you can use the following table to see the temperatures/marks to use. (You can also use this table if you want to convert an old recipe that says something like, "Bake in a warm oven....") Note that the Celsius temperatures are the conventional equivalents, not the precise conversions. For the formulas for precise conversions, see Oven Temperatures and Formulas on page 155.

Oven temperature equivalents

Fahrenheit (°F)	Celsius (°C)	Gas Mark	Descriptive Term
150 to 194	66 to 90	NA	Drying
200 to 230	93 to 110	1/4	Very slow/very low
248 to 266	120 to 130	1/2 or .5	Very slow/very low
275	140	1	Slow/low
300	150	2	Slow/low
325	160	3	Moderately slow/warm
350	180	4	Moderate/medium
375	190	5	Moderate/moderately hot
400	200	6	Moderately hot
425	210	7	Hot
450	220	8	Hot/very hot
475	240	9	Very hot
500	260	10	Extremely hot

Recommended Kitchen Appliances
• •

Plenty of cookbooks write about the basic baking and cooking tools (cutting boards, measuring cups and spoons, baking pans, and the like), so I won't repeat that information. However, I'd like to say a few words about kitchen appliances.

First, you don't need them. Many of this book's recipes were created before our modern appliances were invented. Also, when I was younger and had fewer tools, I found it dismaying to be given instructions that called for a particular appliance that I didn't have. As a good baker and cook, I could come up with a workaround, but I didn't think I should have had to. Keeping this in mind, I did my best to write the instructions to avoid specifying any appliance-based method. (In the computer software industry, we would call this approach "tool agnostic.")

For example, if the instructions are to melt chocolate, I leave it up to you to decide whether you want to melt it in a double boiler, the microwave, or a small pan on direct heat. If the instructions say to cream butter and sugar together, you get to decide whether you want to use a wooden spoon or an electric mixer. Cut butter into flour? Use your pasty cutter, two knives, or your food processor. (In recipes where an appliance makes a hard job super easy, I specify using that appliance.)

However, appliances are huge conveniences and can save you a lot of time and elbow grease. You can still make everything in this cookbook with only the basic cook's tools, no appliances (aside from a stove, oven, and refrigerator), but if you're fortunate, you don't have to. Here are my favorite appliances.

A **stand mixer**, such as a KitchenAid, is a big time saver. You'll find many choices of stand mixer brands and style. In the several Facebook baking groups I belong to, almost everyone recommends KitchenAid. I bought mine in 1996 and it's worked beautifully ever since.

A good, **sturdy blender** is also helpful. I love my Vitamix, but you can find a few other good options. **Immersion blenders** are also useful.

The great chefs and cooks of the past didn't have **food processors** and they didn't need them. But a food processor can turn a ten-minute chore into a quick one-minute task. Before I got a food processor, I was skeptical about their usefulness. But then I received my first food processor in 2015 as a Mother's Day gift, and I love it. I still do some cooking tasks by hand that my food processor could do, but a food processor is brilliant for cutting butter into flour for pie crusts and other such tasks. Use yours as desired for any recipe that makes sense to use it.

For true luxury, if your budget allows, consider purchasing an **ice cream machine** that has a built-in compressor, such as the Lello 4080 Musso Lussino 1.5-quart ice cream maker. With one of these, you can have fresh ice cream in less than an hour. I bought my Lello in the late 1990s and my family thought I was nuts for spending that much money on an appliance. I've never regretted it, and neither have they. You'll find some ice cream recipes in this cookbook that I would never have created if I hadn't bought that machine.

Designed for Readability

I designed this cookbook to be highly readable. I used lots of space; put only one recipe on each page (some recipes take two or more pages); and used a clear and legible font. Although the font hasn't been officially tested for readability for dyslexia, my research shows that it shares many of the same characteristics with fonts that have been tested as more readable by people with dyslexia. I looked into fonts specifically for dyslexia, but none of them serve a cookbook's needs (such as supporting fractions).

In addition, to help you keep track of where you are in a recipe, I gave each action its own step. For example, creaming butter and sugar is one action and one step. Adding the vanilla is a new step.

This approach can make it seem as though all but the simplest recipes in this book have many more steps than similar recipes you find elsewhere, but they don't. Those other recipes have just as many steps, but they group many steps into one step to make the recipe less intimidating. (And sometimes to save page space.) That's an okay approach, but the downside is that it's easy to miss a step when each paragraph contains so many instructions.

Acknowledgments

This book wouldn't exist without the recipes passed down from my ancestors or shared by family members, friends, co-workers, acquaintances, and complete strangers, all of whom were happy to share. My thanks to them.

Bryan Muñoz gets my thanks for asking me, "So when are we going to see your cookbook in print?" That was the final encouragement I needed. Here it is, my friend. It turned into two cookbooks; this one, which has most of my favorite desserts, and a second one with a variety of mostly savory recipes (plus the favorite dessert recipes I didn't include in this book).

Morgan Harrington gets my thanks for her enthusiastic willingness to help out in any way. Thanks, Morgan, for the cover photo shoot in my kitchen, and for your expert Adobe Photoshop *fu*.

Frances Buran, one of the best copy editors and proofreaders I've ever had the pleasure to work with, proofed the book and the index. Thank you! Any remaining errors are mine.

When I was struggling with some knotty fraction problems (and a cookbook is *filled* with fractions), Jos Buivenga, the creator of the elegantly friendly and readable Museo and Museo Slab fonts I use in this cookbook, came to my aid late on a Saturday night. Jos makes great fonts; I use his Fontin and Fontin SmallCaps on the cover. (I used Laura Worthington's lovely and appropriately named Ganache font for the recipe names, and Missy Meyer's equally appropriately named Breakfast Pastry for the decorative letters in the headnotes, index, and on the back cover.)

Mehmed Pasic, thank you so much for your generous heart and your beautifully professional work creating the Kindle version!

Thank you, Joan Whitman and Delores Simon, for your fantastically useful *Recipes into Type: A Handbook for Cookbook Writers and Editors* (HarperCollins, 1993). Though I didn't follow all your advice: "Celsius" has won over "centigrade" since you first published, and my recipe titles, though informative, are practical and straightforward (as I am), not "inviting and even [with] a little romance."

My thanks to you, the purchaser of this book, for taking a leap of faith by buying this small press cookbook. I would have created this book even if nobody bought it. Your support puts the icing on the cake.

Cakes and Cupcakes

This chapter shares many of my family's very favorite cake recipes. Some of these recipes go back in my family a few generations. Others were shared with me by friends and co-workers, or I found in magazines or newspapers, tried, loved, adapted, and kept. For cake frosting and icing recipes, see *Frostings and Sweet Sauces* (starting on page 103).

Cakes come in three basic types: butter (or creamed) cakes, sponge cakes, and chiffon cakes. Out of these three basic types have arisen a delicious multitude of variations.

- **Butter cakes** are made with butter (or some other fat, such as mayonnaise) and baking powder or baking soda for leavening. Most of the recipes in this cookbook are butter cakes.
- **Sponge cakes** are made with lots of eggs or egg whites, which provide the leavening.
- **Chiffon cakes** are like sponge cakes, but contain some fat (aside from that present in egg yolks) and more eggs.

Cake Baking Tips

One of the keys to making the perfect cake is to have all ingredients at room temperature unless the recipe specifically states otherwise. Also, **don't use an electric mixer** in any cake or cupcake recipe unless specified in the recipe; instead, do it the old-fashioned way and mix by hand. The cake will be tenderer and will rise higher.

Cake Pans: Sizes and Materials Matter

The amount of batter a recipe makes will fit in a certain size of pan. But you can substitute differently sized pans that hold the same volume. For example, a recipe that makes enough batter for a 13" x 9" pan will also fill two 9" round cake pans and vice versa.

For all recipes in this chapter that call for a Bundt pan, the pans are 10" unless otherwise noted. Before filling a Bundt pan, butter it thoroughly. After baking, allow the pan to cool completely before attempting to remove the cake; the cake will come out of the pan much more easily that way. If you use a Bundt pan often enough, invest in a heavy-weight one.

You can make cupcakes from most cake recipes and vice versa. Cupcakes take much less time to bake than cakes (often just 12 minutes), so if you're using a cake recipe to make cupcakes, test the cupcakes for doneness much sooner than you would for the cake.

Unless otherwise specified, and with three size exceptions, the cake pans I used for these recipes are metal. If you are using a glass baking pan, see *Adjusting Baking Temperatures and Times* on page 16 for baking tips. I used glass pans to test all recipes that call for 8" x 8", 11" x 7", and 13" x 9" pans.

Here's a short table of the most common pan sizes used in this cookbook. For a more complete table, see *Weights and Measures* (page 149).

Baking pans by size and volume (short table)

Size in inches	Approximate size in centimeters	Approximate capacity in US cups	Approximate capacity in liters or milliliters
Bundt and tube pans			
10 x 4 Bundt or tube pan	25 x 10	16	3.8 liters
Heart-shaped pans			
8 x 2½	20 x 6	8	1.9 liters
Jelly roll pans			
15½ x 10½ x 1	39 x 27 x 2.5	10	2.4 liters
17½ x 12½ x 1	44 x 32 x 2.5	12	2.8 liters
Loaf pans			
8 x 4 x 2½	20 x 10 x 6	4	948 ml
9 x 5 x 3	23 x 13 x 8	8	1.9 liters
Muffin tins (sizes are per well)			
1¾ x ¾ (mini)	4.5 x 2	⅛ (per well)	30 ml
2¾ x 1½ (standard)	7 x 4	½ (per well)	118 ml
Pie pans			
9 x 2	23 x 5	6	1.4 liters
9½ x 2 (deep dish)	24 x 5	7	1.7 liters
Rectangular pans			
8 x 8	20 x 20	6	1.4 liters
9 x 9	23 x 23	8	1.9 liters
11 x 7 x 2	28 x 18 x 5	8	1.9 liters
13 x 9 x 2	33 x 29 x 5	14	3.3 liters
Round pans (cake and springform)			
8 x 2 cake or springform	20 x 5	6	1.4 liters
9 x 1½ cake	23 x 4	6	1.4 liters
9 x 2 cake	23 x 5	8	1.9 liters
9 x 2½ springform	23 X 6	10	2.4 liters
Square pans			
8 x 8 x 2	20 x 20 x 5	8	1.9 liters
9 x 9 x 2	23 x 23 x 5	10	2.4 liters

About "Greasing" and Flouring Those Pans

Many recipes call for greasing (and sometimes flouring) a pan. In the old days, "grease" meant whatever fat you had on hand—butter, lard, bacon grease, oil, or shortening. Today, you can still use any of those, and you can also use cooking spray. I've found that coconut oil is a splendid substitute for "grease," and that's what I usually use. (Though butter is a second choice.) If you haven't experimented with coconut oil, I recommend giving it a try.

"Flouring" a pan means to lightly dust the pan's bottom (and sometimes sides) with all-purpose flour. When baking chocolate cakes, I use cocoa powder instead of flour. (This is an old family secret—a secret many families share—for subtly intensifying the taste of chocolate cakes.)

Adjusting Baking Temperatures and Times

If you're baking in glass pans, reduce the oven temperature by 25°; if using a convection oven, reduce the oven temperature by 25° and reduce the cooking time by about 30%. Don't add the two reductions. For example, if a recipe calls for baking a cake at 350° for 30 minutes, and you are baking it in a glass pan in a convection oven, bake it in the convection oven at 325° for 20 minutes, then check for doneness. You may need to cook it longer anyway, but it's better to check sooner and have to cook it a little more than to end up with a sad, dry, overcooked cake.

Testing Cakes for Doneness

To test a cake for doneness, insert a cake tester or a toothpick near the center; the tester should come out clean. Unless otherwise stated in a recipe, this is what a recipe means when it says "test a cake for doneness."

Boston Cream Pie

Prep/cook time: 1 hour   Makes one two-layer 8" cake

Boston Cream Pie is really a cake with a sweet, soft custard filling (the Boston cream from which it gets its name). It's a bit fussy for everyday, but makes an impressive two-layer dessert for special occasions. The custard is usually vanilla flavored; I've included instructions for making a chocolate version as well. The recipes for the custard and icing follow the main recipe. Fun fact: Boston Cream Pie became the Massachusetts state dessert in 1996.

Ingredients for the Cake

2 cups cake flour
2 teaspoons baking powder
½ teaspoon salt
½ cup unsalted butter
1 cup granulated sugar

3 large egg yolks
1 teaspoon vanilla extract or 1 teaspoon lemon zest
¾ cup whole milk

Ingredients for the Custard Filling

1½ cups whole milk
1 vanilla bean or 1½ teaspoons vanilla extract
2 to 4 ounces semisweet chocolate (optional; to make a chocolate filling)

½ cup granulated sugar
¼ cup all-purpose flour
3 to 4 well-beaten large egg yolks or 2 whole large eggs and 2 yolks

Ingredients for the Chocolate Icing

1 tablespoon unsalted butter
4 ounces semisweet chocolate
6 tablespoons heavy cream

1½ cups powdered sugar (or to taste)
1 teaspoon vanilla extract

Making the Cake Layers

1 Mix cake flour, baking powder, and salt. Set aside.
2 Cream butter, then gradually add sugar. Cream together until light.

3   Beat egg yolks one at a time into the butter mixture.
4   Add vanilla or lemon zest to butter mixture.
5   Add the flour mixture to the creamed mixture alternately with the milk, stirring after each addition.
6   Bake in two greased 8" layer pans at 350° for about 25 minutes. While the cake bakes, make the custard filling and the icing.

Making the Custard Filling

1   Add vanilla bean or vanilla extract to milk and scald the milk (180°). **If making a chocolate filling**, melt the chocolate in the milk when scalding it.
2   Place remaining ingredients in a double boiler and beat until light.
3   If you used a vanilla bean, remove it from the scalded milk.
4   Gradually add the scalded milk to the mixture in the double boiler. Stir until well blended.
5   Cook, stirring constantly, until the mixture starts to thicken.
6   Remove from heat and continue to stir to release the steam and prevent the milk from developing a skin.
7   Cool before using.

Making the Chocolate Icing

1   Melt butter and chocolate in a double boiler.
2   Add heavy cream and blend well.
3   Stir in powdered sugar until icing is smooth and as sweet as desired.

Putting It Together

1   When the cake is done baking and cooled, place one layer on a plate. Cover with all the custard filling. Leave the sides exposed.
2   Place the second layer on top.
3   Cover the top layer with the chocolate icing while the icing is still warm. Allow some to drip down the sides.

Cherry Cake

Prep/cook time: 45 minutes   Makes a two-layer 9" cake

This recipe came from Mildred Kelly, who was my stepfather's mother. It was already quite old when she gave it to my mother in the 1960s. Judging from the wording in the recipe, I believe it dates back to the pioneer times in the 1800s. I've modernized the instructions and standardized the ingredients. Frost with Basic Buttercream Frosting (page 105).

½ cup unsalted butter
1½ cups granulated sugar
2¼ cups all-purpose flour
3 teaspoons baking powder
¼ cup cherry juice
½ cup whole milk

2 large eggs, separated, or 2 large egg whites
⅓ cup fresh or canned cherries, cut up (reserve some cherries for the top)
½ cup finely chopped nuts

1 Preheat oven to 350°. Grease and flour two 9" round cake pans.
2 Cream butter and sugar together.
3 Add egg yolks to butter mixture.
4 Combine flour and baking powder and set aside.
5 Combine cherry juice and milk.
6 Add flour mixture and juice mixture alternately to the butter mixture.
7 Add cherries and nuts.
8 Beat the egg whites to soft peaks. Fold into batter.
9 Bake at 350° for 25 minutes. Let cool. Remove from pans.
10 When cool, frost, then garnish with cherries.

Chocolate Cardamom Cake

Prep/cook time: 1 hour 10 minutes   Makes a two-layer 9" cake

This family favorite makes a perfect chocolate cake with a hint of cardamom. Because mayonnaise is mostly oil and egg, it substitutes for butter in this recipe. You can find the rich, dark, flavorful Valrhona cocoa (my favorite Dutch process cocoa) at ChocoSphere.com. You can use a different brand of cocoa powder, but it must be Dutch process. The cardamom and the chocolate chips are an optional but fantastic addition, especially if you make cupcakes from this recipe. You can add more cardamom, but don't be tempted to add a lot—cardamom's flavor intensifies with time. This recipe halves well.

2 cups organic unbleached all-purpose flour
$2/3$ cup plus 2 tablespoons Valrhona cocoa powder
1 teaspoon baking soda
$1/4$ teaspoon baking powder
$3/4$ teaspoon ground cardamom

$1 2/3$ cups organic granulated sugar
4 large organic eggs
1 teaspoon vanilla extract
1 cup organic mayonnaise
$1 1/3$ cup filtered water
$1 2/3$ cups bittersweet (60% cacao) chocolate chips

1 Butter the bottoms of two 9" layer cake pans. Then, use the 2 tablespoons of cocoa to coat the bottom and sides of the pans.
2 By hand, mix the flour, cocoa, baking soda, baking powder, and cardamom in a small bowl and set aside.
3 In large bowl, beat sugar, eggs, and vanilla for 3 minutes or until light and fluffy. (If using a mixer, mix at high speed.)
4 Beat in mayonnaise. (If using a mixer, mix at low speed.)
5 **Switch to mixing the cake by hand.** (If you continue using a mixer, the cake will be tough.) Starting and ending with the flour mixture, add the flour mixture one-fourth at a time, alternating with water. The batter will be *very* liquid. Stir in chocolate chips.
6 Pour batter into pans. Don't overfill the pans—about half-way is good. If you have extra batter, pour it into cupcake or muffin tins.
7 Bake at 350° for 30 to 35 minutes or until cakes test done.
8 Remove from oven and cool 10 minutes in pan. Remove from pans and cool on racks.

Chocolate Decadence Cake

Prep/cook time: 1 hour   Makes one single-layer 9" cake

erve this deeply rich (and gluten-free!) cake in small portions topped with whipped cream.

12 ounces bittersweet chocolate	**2** tablespoons plus 4 tablespoons granulated sugar
½ cup unsalted butter	
8 large eggs, separated	**1** teaspoon vanilla extract
	1 pinch of salt

1   Cut parchment paper to fit the bottom of a 9" springform pan. Butter bottom of pan. Place paper on top of the buttered bottom, then butter the paper.
2   In a heavy saucepan, melt chocolate with butter, stirring constantly until smooth. Remove melted chocolate from the heat.
3   Beat egg yolks a few minutes with the vanilla and the 2 tablespoons sugar.
4   Using a wire whip, quickly stir beaten egg yolks into the chocolate mixture.
5   Place chocolate mixture in a large bowl.
6   In a separate bowl, beat egg whites with the salt, gradually adding the remaining 4 tablespoons sugar, beating until soft peaks form.
7   Put egg whites on top of chocolate mixture. Carefully and lightly whisk whites into the chocolate, being careful not to overstir.
8   Spread batter into prepared pan and bake at 350° for 30 to 35 minutes or until it is cracked on top and a toothpick comes out clean from the center.
9   Cool on wire rack. The cake will shrink as it cools.
10 Remove pan and loosen cake from paper.

Chocolate Pound Cake

Prep/cook time: 1 hour 40 minutes   Makes one 12-cup Bundt cake

Even if you aren't a fan of pound cake, this one tastes wonderful. It's perfect for serving at tea time. Try it sprinkled with powdered sugar or glazed with Hot Gingerbread Icing (page 116).

1 cup unsalted butter	**3** teaspoons baking powder
3 cups granulated sugar	**1** teaspoon salt
1 tablespoon vanilla extract	**1½** cups whole milk
3 cups all-purpose flour	**3** large eggs
1 cup Dutch process cocoa powder	**¼** cup evaporated milk

1 Grease and flour a 12-cup Bundt pan
2 Cream butter, sugar, and vanilla until fluffy.
3 Combine dry ingredients and add alternately with milk to butter mixture. Beat 3 minutes.
4 Add eggs one at a time and beat in well.
5 Add evaporated milk. Beat 2 minutes.
6 Pour into a 10" Bundt pan and bake for 1½ hours or until cake tests done.
7 Cool 10 to 15 minutes in pan.
8 Turn out onto wire rack and cool completely.

Chocolate Snack Cake

Prep/cook time: 1 hour   Makes one 8" square cake

T his rich, moist cake tastes great without any frosting. At most, just sprinkle powdered sugar on top. It's excellent with tea or coffee.

1⅓ cups all-purpose flour	1 cup water
1 cup packed brown sugar	⅓ cup vegetable oil
¼ cup natural cocoa powder	1 teaspoon vinegar
1 teaspoon baking soda	¾ teaspoon vanilla extract
¼ teaspoon salt	½ cup chocolate chips

1   Preheat oven to 350°. Grease and flour an 8" x 8" square cake pan.
2   In a medium mixing bowl, combine flour, sugar, cocoa, baking soda, and salt.
3   Add water, oil, vinegar, and vanilla to the flour mixture; beat until smooth.
4   Pour batter into prepared pan. Sprinkle chocolate chips over top.
5   Bake for 35 to 40 minutes or until cake tests done.
6   Cool in pan for ten minutes on a wire rack.

Cocoa Apple Cake

Prep/cook time: 1 hour 30 minutes   Makes one 12-cup Bundt cake

This moist, tasty apple cake has a very light cocoa flavor. It's an excellent way to use that abundant apple harvest.

2 cups granulated sugar	**1** teaspoon ground cinnamon
1 cup unsalted butter	**1** teaspoon ground allspice
3 large eggs, beaten	**1** cup finely chopped walnuts
½ cup water	**½** cup chocolate chips
2½ cups all-purpose flour	**2** cups peeled, cored, and
2 tablespoons natural cocoa	grated apples
powder	**1** tablespoon vanilla extract
1 teaspoon baking soda	

1   Prepare a 12-cup Bundt pan or a 10" loose-bottom tube pan by greasing well.
2   In a large bowl, cream sugar and butter together.
3   Add eggs and water. Stir well.
4   In a separate bowl, combine flour, cocoa, baking soda, cinnamon, and allspice.
5   Add flour mixture to egg/butter mixture and mix well.
6   Fold in walnuts, chocolate chips, apples, and vanilla.
7   Spoon into prepared pan.
8   Bake at 325° for 60 to 70 minutes or until cake tests done.
9   Cool cake in pan completely before removing from pan.

Date Coffee Cake

Prep/cook time: 45 minutes   Makes one 13" x 9" cake

According to FoodTimeline.org, ancient honey cakes evolved into what we think of as coffee cake today: a sweet, slightly dry cake to be served with coffee. The custom of eating a sweet cake with coffee probably began sometime in Northern and Central Europe in the 1600s and came to America with Dutch, German, and Scandinavian immigrants. This delicious coffee cake has no added sugar; it gets its sweetness from the bananas and dates. It doesn't need frosting.

⅓ cup mashed banana
½ cup unsalted butter, softened
3 large eggs
1 teaspoon vanilla extract
1¼ cups water
3 cups all-purpose flour

1 teaspoon baking soda
2 teaspoons baking powder
1½ cups plus ½ cup chopped dates
⅓ cup chopped walnuts or almonds
⅓ cup flaked coconut

1   Grease and flour a 13" x 9" pan.
2   Combine banana and butter and beat until creamy.
3   Add eggs, vanilla, and water; mix well.
4   Add flour, baking soda, and baking powder; mix well.
5   Stir in the 1½ cups dates.
6   Spoon batter into prepared pan.
7   Combine remaining ½ cup dates with the nuts and coconut. Sprinkle over batter.
8   Bake at 350° for 20 to 25 minutes or until a knife inserted in the middle comes out clean.

Dolce Torinese

Prep/cook time: 6 hours (includes 5   Makes one 9" loaf cake
hours chill time)

Susan Caron, an Italian neighbor in Tucson in the early 1980s, said this recipe
for a no-bake rum-soaked chocolate terrine had been in her family for years.
The unmolding step is the hardest part of the recipe; a hinged loaf pan makes it easier. Serve with whipped cream.

8 ounces semisweet chocolate
or 1⅓ cups chocolate chips
⅓ cup rum
½ cup unsalted butter
2 tablespoons plus ⅓ cup
powdered sugar
2 large eggs, separated

1½ cup finely chopped
almonds or hazelnuts
1 pinch of salt
12 butter biscuits (Petite Buerre
or Social Tea brand) or
homemade shortbread
cookies, cut into 1-inch
squares

1   Lightly grease a 1½ quart loaf pan (or line pan with plastic wrap).
2   Melt the chocolate in a medium saucepan over low heat.
3   Stir rum into the melted chocolate. Remove from heat and cool
to room temperature.
4   Cream butter and the 2 tablespoons powdered sugar together
until light.
5   Beat egg yolks into the butter mixture.
6   Stir nuts and cooled chocolate into the butter/sugar/egg mixture.
7   In a separate bowl, beat egg whites to soft peaks.
8   Fold egg whites into chocolate mixture.
9   When no streaks of white show, gently fold in the cut-up biscuits.
10 Spoon into the loaf pan and smooth the top with a spatula. Cover
tightly with plastic wrap and refrigerate or freeze for at least 4
hours or until loaf is very firm.
11 One hour before serving, unmold: run a sharp knife around the
edges and dip the bottom of the pan into hot water for a few
seconds. Pat dry, then invert onto a chilled platter. Once the loaf
is on the plate, smooth top and sides.
12 Refrigerate again for one hour. Just before serving, sift the
remaining ⅓ cup powdered sugar over the top.

Food of the Gods Carrot Cake

Prep/cook time: 1 hour Makes one 8" x 8" cake

A Facebook acquaintance shared the original version of this recipe, saying it was the best they've ever had. "Best" is relative, because we each have our own preferred type of carrot cake, but it's an excellent cake and the only one my daughter likes. She says carrot cake always tastes of "walnuts and regret," but she likes this version. The Facebook acquaintance found the original in "an old Grange cookbook." I adapted it to my tastes (for example, by adding cocoa and a lot more spices, and substituting brown sugar for some of the granulated sugar). I also put the ingredients in order and rewrote the instructions so they're more sensible and comprehensible. And I changed the pan size, because the size called for in the original recipe made a *very* flat cake. The classic frosting for carrot cake is Cream Cheese Frosting (page 112).

1 cup all-purpose flour
¾ cup granulated sugar
¼ cup packed brown sugar
1 teaspoon baking soda
¼ teaspoon salt
1 teaspoon Dutch process cocoa
1 teaspoon ground cinnamon
½ teaspoon ground ginger
¼ teaspoon ground allspice
¼ teaspoon ground mace (optional; some people dislike the sharpness of mace)
⅛ teaspoon ground cloves
¾ cup avocado oil
2 large eggs, beaten
1½ cups finely grated carrots
½ cup chocolate chips (optional)

1 Preheat oven to 350°. Grease and flour an 8" x 8" baking pan.
2 Combine flour, sugar, baking soda, salt, cocoa, and spices and blend well.
3 Stir in oil and eggs and beat together for 5 minutes.
4 Add carrots and mix well.
5 Stir in chocolate chips.
6 Pour into prepared baking pan. Spread batter evenly.
7 Bake for 30 minutes or until just done when tested with a toothpick. Don't over bake or cake will be dry.
8 Remove from oven and cool in pan for ten minutes.
9 Turn out on a rack and cool completely.

Fudgy Chocolate Layer Cake

Prep/cook time: 40 minutes   Makes one two-layer 9" cake

I love baking with buttermilk; through the magic of chemistry, buttermilk makes cakes tender. (Just as it does with pancakes.) Try this cake with Bittersweet Chocolate Frosting (page 106).

1¾ cups all-purpose flour	⅔ cup granulated sugar
1 cup natural cocoa powder	⅔ cup firmly packed dark
1¼ teaspoons baking soda	brown sugar
⅛ teaspoon salt	2 teaspoons vanilla extract
¾ cup unsalted butter,	2 large eggs
softened	1½ cups buttermilk

1   Preheat oven to 350° and line the bottoms of two 9" round cake pans with waxed or parchment paper. Grease the paper and sides of pans. Dust paper with cocoa.
2   Combine flour, cocoa, baking soda, and salt.
3   In another bowl, cream butter with sugars.
4   Add vanilla and eggs to butter/sugar mixture.
5   Alternately mix flour mixture and buttermilk into butter/sugar mixture until just blended.
6   Divide batter equally between pans.
7   Bake cakes 25 to 30 minutes or until they test clean.
8   Remove from oven. Cool on wire racks for 10 minutes.
9   Remove from pans. Cool completely.

Gingerbread

Prep/cook time: 1 hour   Makes one 13" x 9" cake

My mother's recipe, this fine-crumbed and tangy gingerbread is a light-textured cake, not a bread.

1½ cups granulated sugar
½ cup unsalted butter
2 large eggs
1 cup whole milk
3 cups all-purpose flour
2 teaspoons baking powder

½ teaspoon salt
2 tablespoons ground
    cinnamon
2 tablespoons ground ginger
½ teaspoon ground allspice

1   In a medium bowl, cream sugar, butter, and eggs together.
2   In another medium bowl, combine the flour, baking powder, salt, and spices.
3   Add the flour mixture to the egg/butter mixture.
4   Pour into a 13" x 9" pan and bake at 300° for 45 minutes.
5   Remove from oven and cool until just warm to the touch. While the gingerbread is cooling, make the Hot Gingerbread Icing (page 116) or the Orange Icing (page 118).
6   While still warm, top with icing and serve.

Hi-Hat Cupcakes

Prep/cook time: 3 to 4 hours   Makes 24 cupcakes

In music, a hi-hat is the combination of a cymbal and its stand. In cooking, hi-hats are delicious cupcakes piled high with a marshmallow topping that is then coated with chocolate. Some people substitute basic buttercream frosting for the marshmallow topping, but the results are a little too dense for my taste. This recipe uses a chocolate cupcake recipe as a base, though any recipe that makes a fairly firm cake/cupcake will do. The recipe is a lot of work, so tackle it when you have time, patience, and enthusiasm. You may wish to recruit a friend to help. As Prue Leith says, "The results are worth the calories" (and effort).

Ingredients for the Cupcakes

3 ounces unsweetened chocolate, chopped
1 cup all-purpose flour
1/2 teaspoon baking powder
1/2 teaspoon baking soda
1/4 teaspoon salt

1/2 cup unsalted butter, softened
1 1/4 cups granulated sugar
2 large eggs
1 teaspoon vanilla extract
1/2 cup sour cream
1/2 cup water

Ingredients for the Marshmallow Topping

1 3/4 cups granulated sugar
1/4 cup water
3 large egg whites

1/4 teaspoon cream of tartar
1 teaspoon vanilla extract

Ingredients for the Chocolate Coating

2 cups semisweet chocolate chips or 12 ounces chopped semisweet chocolate

2 1/2 tablespoons melted coconut oil (or light vegetable oil)

Making the Cupcakes

1   Preheat the oven to 350°. Prepare cupcake tins with liners.
2   Melt the chocolate on low heat. Set aside to cool slightly.

3   Combine the flour, baking powder, baking soda, and salt in a medium bowl and set aside.

4   You can use an electric mixer for the next few steps. Place the butter and sugar in a large bowl and mix until blended, about 2 minutes.

5   On low speed, mix in the melted chocolate.

6   On medium speed, add eggs one at a time, mixing until each is blended.

7   Add vanilla and beat 1 minute.

8   Mix in the sour cream until no white streaks remain.

9   Hand-mix in half the flour mixture, mixing well. Add the water, then the remaining flour mixture. Mix until the batter is smooth.

10 Fill each cupcake liner with ⅓ cup of batter, to about ⅛ inch below the top of the liner. Bake just until the top feels firm and the cupcakes test done (about 20 minutes). Remove from oven and set aside to cool.

Making the Marshmallow Topping

1   While the cupcakes are cooling, make the topping. Combine the sugar, water, egg whites, and cream of tartar in the top of a 2-quart (or larger) double boiler and, before you start the heat under the double boiler, beat with a handheld electric mixer on high speed about 1 minute.

2   Bring the water in the bottom of the double boiler to a bare simmer and beat the mixture on high speed until it forms stiff peaks when you stop the beaters and lift them out (about 12 minutes). If there were a way to use a stand mixer for this step, I would, because it is tedious standing at the stove for 12 minutes with a hand mixer. Plus your hands get tired. And it's noisy.

3   Remove the top container of the double boiler from the water. Quickly add the vanilla extract to the mixture. Continue beating for 2 minutes. The filling will become firmer as it cools. It will also make a big mess, so work quickly from this point.

Topping the Cupcakes

1   Spoon the marshmallow topping into a large pastry bag or cake decorating gun with a large tip. (I *highly* recommend the gun over the pastry bag.) Starting in the center of each cupcake, pipe a spiral, moving out to the edge, creating a mound much like a soft-serve ice cream cone. Aim for a height of about 2 inches.

2   Place the filled cupcakes on a plate or cutting board and
     refrigerate, uncovered, while you immediately clean up
     everything the marshmallow touched. Don't let the marshmallow
     dry on anything unless you want to chip it off with a jackhammer
     later. The good news is, the fresh marshmallow cleans up easily
     with just warm water.

Adding the Chocolate Coating

1   To make the chocolate coating, combine the chocolate and
     coconut oil and melt gently. Use a double boiler or direct heat; if
     you use direct heat, keep it low and watch it like a hawk to keep
     the chocolate from burning or seizing.
2   Place the chocolate coating in a small, narrow container—one
     with room to dip the cupcakes—and cool for about 15 minutes.
3   When the coating has cooled, hold each cupcake by its bottom
     and swiftly dip the marshmallow top into the chocolate coating.
     Make sure you coat the whole top.
4   Set the cupcakes aside for 15 minutes, then refrigerate for
     another 30 minutes or until the coating hardens.
5   Cover and refrigerate for another 2 hours to make sure the
     coating is set, or serve immediately.

Honey Spice Cupcakes

Prep/cook time: 30 minutes   Makes 24 cupcakes

T hese cupcakes were inspired by a honey cake recipe in *The Honey Kitchen* (Dadant & Sons, 1980), a cookbook I purchased when I first started keeping bees. Because they're unusual, these cupcakes are popular at potluck dinners; plus cupcakes make a tidy and easy serving. The Basic Buttercream Frosting (page 105) is a nice complement to the spices.

2 cups all-purpose flour
½ teaspoon salt
1 teaspoon baking soda
¾ teaspoon ground cloves
¾ teaspoon ground allspice
¾ teaspoon ground cinnamon

1 cup packed brown sugar
½ cup unsalted butter
1 cup honey
3 large eggs
1 cup sour cream

1   Prepare 1-cup cupcake tins by either greasing with coconut oil or lining with cupcake liners. (By "1-cup cupcake tins," I mean tins that can hold one cup in each well.)
2   Combine flour, salt, baking soda, and spices. Mix very well. Set aside.
3   Cream butter and brown sugar together.
4   Add honey and eggs to butter mixture.
5   Starting with the flour mixture, alternately add flour and sour cream to the butter/sugar mixture until well mixed.
6   Fill cupcake cups half full.
7   Bake at 350° for 15 minutes.
8   Remove from oven and remove from baking tins immediately.
9   Cool completely, then frost.

Molten Chocolate Lava Cakes

Prep/cook time: 30 minutes   Makes 6 servings

L ava cakes are individual-sized cakes (typically chocolate) with a hot, liquid core. The core is traditionally chocolate, though people have branched out to molten peanut butter cores. Whatever the filling, you serve these hot from the oven, topped with whipped cream or with a side of vanilla ice cream.

4 ounces semisweet baking chocolate
½ cup unsalted butter
1 cup powdered sugar
2 large egg yolks plus 2 large eggs, lightly beaten
6 tablespoons all-purpose flour
¼ teaspoon salt
1 cup heavy cream

1   Preheat oven to 425°. Prepare six half-cup ramekins by buttering them thoroughly. Be sure to get butter into the edges.
2   Melt the chocolate and butter together in a double boiler. Stir until reasonably well mixed.
3   Put sugar in a medium mixing bowl, then drizzle chocolate in, mixing well.
4   Add egg yolk/egg mixture and mix well.
5   Stir in flour and salt; mix well.
6   Evenly distribute batter into the ramekins. They'll be about half full.
7   Bake for 12 to 14 minutes or until the cakes have risen and are cracking slightly on the top. Better to err on the side of underdone with these.
8   Remove from oven and let stand for a minute, then run a knife or small spatula around the outer edges to loosen. Carefully remove and place right-side up in an individual serving plate or bowl. Serve immediately.

Mug Cake

Prep/cook time: 10 minutes   Makes 1 mug cake

T ry this fun recipe with children—with supervision, of course. Or when you're in the mood for chocolate cake but don't have the time or inclination to make a whole one. Essentially, you place all ingredients in a large ceramic mug, then cook it in a microwave oven. It makes a delightful mini-cake that slides out of the mug onto your plate, much like the breads that are cooked in coffee cans.

4 tablespoons all-purpose flour
4 tablespoons granulated sugar
2 tablespoons cocoa powder
1 large egg, lightly beaten
3 tablespoons whole milk

3 tablespoons unsalted butter
3 tablespoons chocolate chips
⅛ teaspoon vanilla extract
1 large (12-ounce) ceramic mug

1   Add flour, sugar, and cocoa to mug and mix very well.
2   Add egg and mix well.
3   Add the chocolate chips and vanilla extract, and mix well.
4   Place mug in microwave and cook for 3 minutes at 1,000 watts. The cake will rise over the edge of the mug.
5   Remove from microwave and allow to cool for 2 to 3 minutes.
6   Slide cake out onto a plate or into a bowl and enjoy. Or just eat from the mug. Eat carefully! It may have hot pockets.

Orange Layer Cake

Prep/cook time: 45 minutes   Makes a two-layer 9" cake

Collected in the 1970s from an unremembered source, this unusual cake is a unique addition to parties, pot lucks, work, or home. Delicious with Orange Icing (page 118).

2¼ cups all-purpose flour
1½ cups granulated sugar
2 teaspoons baking powder
¼ teaspoon baking soda
1 teaspoon salt

¼ cup orange juice
¾ cup whole milk
½ cup unsalted butter
zest of one orange

1   Mix together flour, sugar, baking powder, baking soda, and salt.
2   Combine the orange juice and milk and mix well.
3   Add butter, orange zest, and ⅔ cup of the orange/milk mixture to the flour mix. Beat until smooth.
4   Add the remaining ⅓ cup of the orange/milk mixture. Beat a few more minutes.
5   Bake in two 9" layer pans for 30 minutes at 350°.
6   Remove from pans immediately. Cool completely on racks before frosting.

Poppy Seed Cake

Prep/cook time: 1 hour 10 minutes   Makes one 12-cup Bundt cake

A long-time favorite. I love the crunch of the tiny poppy seeds. My InDesign instructor, whose daughter was a professional golfer, told me athletes must avoid poppy seed cake because eating poppy seeds can cause you to test positive for opiates. Serve unfrosted with slightly sweetened whipped cream.

2½ cups granulated sugar
1 cup avocado oil (or other
   mild cooking oil)
3 large eggs
1½ teaspoons vanilla extract

3 cups all-purpose flour
3 tablespoons poppy seeds
1½ teaspoons baking powder
½ teaspoon salt
1½ cups whole milk

1 Preheat oven to 350°.
2 Grease and flour a 12-cup Bundt pan.
3 Mix sugar, oil, eggs, and vanilla in a large bowl.
4 Mix flour, poppy seeds, baking powder, and salt separately.
5 Alternately stir the flour mixture and milk into the sugar mixture, beginning and ending with the dry ingredients.
6 Pour batter into the prepared pan and bake until a tester inserted near the center comes out clean (about 50 minutes).
7 Cool 10 to 20 minutes, then remove from pan.

Tender Fudge Layer Cake

Prep/cook time: 1 hour 10 minutes   Makes one two-layer 8" cake

The original version of this delicious recipe, a long-time family favorite, came from the March 1976 issue of *Woman's Day* magazine—which cost "Only 35¢." I changed the leavening so I could use Dutch process cocoa. If you're using Valrhona cocoa powder, reduce the cocoa to ½ cup. This cake is delicious frosted with either the Fluffy Chocolate Buttercream Frosting (page 113) or the Ultimate Chocolate Frosting (page 119).

1¾ cups all-purpose flour
¾ cup Dutch process cocoa
    powder
1 teaspoon baking powder
¾ teaspoon salt
½ cup unsalted butter,
    softened

1⅓ cups granulated sugar
2 large eggs
1 teaspoon vanilla extract
2 ounces unsweetened
    chocolate, melted
1 cup ice water

1   Preheat oven to 350°. Prepare two 8" cake pans by greasing them and lining the bottoms with wax paper.
2   Mix flour, cocoa, baking powder, and salt; set aside.
3   In a large bowl, cream butter, sugar, eggs, and vanilla until fluffy.
4   Stir in melted chocolate.
5   Stir in flour and ice water alternately, blending well after each addition. (If using a mixer, use low speed.)
6   Pour into prepared cake pans.
7   Bake for 30 minutes or until cake tests done.
8   Cool on racks ten minutes.
9   Remove from pans, remove paper, and cool completely before frosting.

Tunnel of Fudge Bundt Cake

Prep/cook time: 2 hours   Makes one 12-cup Bundt cake

An easy cake for how delicious it is. Yes, the frosting goes *into* the batter, where it forms a pudding-like filling. If you want, you can use canned frosting, but I make my own using one of the chocolate frosting recipes from the chapter *Frostings and Sweet Sauces* (page 103).

1½ cups unsalted butter,
    softened
6 large eggs
1⅓ cups granulated sugar

2 cups all-purpose flour
3⅓ cups chocolate frosting
2 cups chopped walnuts

1   Thoroughly grease a 12-cup Bundt pan and set aside.
2   Cream butter.
3   Add eggs, beating well after each.
4   Gradually add sugar and beat until light and fluffy.
5   Stir in flour, frosting, and walnuts.
6   Bake in Bundt pan at 350° for 60 to 65 minutes. Cake is done when crust is dry and brownie-like.
7   Cool 30 minutes; remove from pan.

Wacky Cake

Prep/cook time: 45 minutes   Makes one single-layer 8" square cake

Easy enough for children to make, this moist cake recipe was popular in US schools in the 1960s (though the recipe is even older). It's called "wacky" because you mix the cake directly in the baking pan and it has neither eggs nor butter. You'll find many variations of this recipe; this is mine with a poke-cake flare.

Ingredients for the Cake

1½ cups all-purpose flour
1 cup granulated sugar
¼ cup natural cocoa powder
1 teaspoon baking soda
½ teaspoon salt (optional)

6 tablespoons mild cooking oil
1 tablespoon apple cider
   vinegar
1 cup cold water
1 teaspoon vanilla extract

Ingredients for the Cocoa Honey Icing

1 cup powdered sugar
2 tablespoons cocoa powder
2 tablespoons honey
¼ teaspoon cream of tartar

1½ cups unsalted butter
1 teaspoon vanilla extract
1½ cups whole milk

Making the Cake

1 Combine the dry ingredients in an 8" x 8" baking pan.
2 Create a hole in the center of the dry ingredients, mounding up the sides like a cone volcano that has erupted.
3 Place the oil, vinegar, water, and vanilla in the hole. The combination will start to bubble. Stir well with a fork.
4 Bake at 350° for 30 minutes or until done.
5 Remove from oven and ice immediately.

Making the Cocoa Honey Icing

1 To make the icing, combine all ingredients in a medium saucepan, bring to a boil, and boil for 5 minutes.
2 When cake comes out of the oven, poke holes in the cake and pour the icing over the cake.

Wellesley Fudge Cake

Prep/cook time: 1 hour   Makes a two-layer 8" cake

T his cake and frosting recipe is an old family treasure, dating back to at least the early 1900s. I have a photocopy of the original in some unknown ancestress's handwriting. For historical interest, although I modernized the ingredients, I've reproduced the recipe instructions here (with a few clarifications), so the "I" in this recipe is that long-ago ancestress.

Ingredients for the Cake

½ cup shortening (I use unsalted butter, softened)
½ cup granulated sugar
2 large eggs, beaten
2 cups all-purpose flour
1 teaspoon baking soda

1 teaspoon baking powder
½ teaspoon salt
1 cup sour milk (buttermilk will work)
½ cup cocoa powder
½ cup hot water

Ingredients for the Chocolate Fudge Icing

2 ounces unsweetened baking chocolate
1½ cups granulated sugar
½ cup water

1 tablespoon unsalted butter
¼ teaspoon cream of tartar
1 teaspoon vanilla extract
2 tablespoons heavy cream

Making the Cake

1   Cream shortening. Add sugar and cream thoroughly.
2   Add all beaten eggs.
3   Sift flour once before measuring. Mix and sift flour, soda, baking powder, and salt together, and add to first mixture alternately with the sour milk.
4   Mix cocoa and hot water to form smooth paste and add to batter.
5   Pour into floured tins and bake 30 to 40 minutes—350°—makes 12 servings. Two 8 in. layer cake tins.

Making the Chocolate Fudge Icing

1   Cut chocolate into small pieces. Combine with the sugar, water, and cream of tartar. Stir to mix thoroughly.
2   Place on fire and, *without* stirring, cook to very soft ball stage (234°). Remove from fire and let stand until perfectly cold.
3   Add vanilla and beat until thick enough to hold its shape.
4   Thin slightly with heavy cream so that it will be of the right consistency to spread.
5   Spread between layers and on top.
6   One cup chopped nuts may be added to this icing, if desired.
7   I make frosting first and stir up cake while frosting cools.

Yellow Cardamom Cake

Prep/cook time: 1 hour   Makes a two-layer 9" cake

T his is our all-time-favorite yellow cake. The recipe is in Rose Levy Beranbaum's
The Cake Bible (William Morrow and Company, Inc, 1988). This recipe's pages
in my copy of the book are spattered with egg yolk and cake batter from the many
times I've made this cake for my daughter. Ms. Beranbaum's recipe calls for cake
flour; I use regular flour, and I add cardamom and chocolate chips. This cake is fabu-
lous with the Fluffy Chocolate Buttercream Frosting (page 113).

6 large egg yolks
¼ cup plus ¾ cup whole milk
2¼ teaspoons vanilla extract
3 cups all-purpose flour
1½ cups granulated sugar
4 teaspoons baking powder

¾ teaspoon ground cardamom
¼ teaspoon salt
1½ cups unsalted butter,
    softened
1 cup chocolate chips

1   Preheat oven to 350°. Prepare two 9" cake pans by greasing them
     and lining them with parchment paper. Grease and flour the
     parchment paper. This preparation helps the cake separate from
     the paper and the paper separate from the pan more easily.
2   Mix the egg yolks, the ¼ cup milk, and the vanilla in a small bowl.
3   In a separate bowl, mix the flour, sugar, baking powder,
     cardamom, and salt.
4   Add the butter and the remaining ¾ cup milk to the flour
     mixture. Mix until the flour mixture is moistened, then beat
     reasonably hard for a few minutes. (This is to aerate the batter,
     which develops the cake's structure.)
5   In three batches, gradually add the egg mixture, beating half a
     minute after each addition.
6   Add the chocolate chips.
7   Pour batter into the prepared pans and bake 25 to 35 minutes or
     until the cakes test done. (The cakes should spring back when
     gently pressed in the center.)
8   Remove from over and cool in the pans for 10 minutes, then
     invert onto wire racks. Peel off the parchment paper.

Candy

aking candy can be intimidating, but it doesn't have to be. If you follow a few basic rules, you can succeed consistently.

Many of the recipes in this chapter are one type of fudge or another. Fudge is more forgiving than other types of candy, and some of the fudge recipes are almost foolproof because they rely on specific ingredients to take the place of fussier cooking.

Making Sugar-Based Candies

When making fudge or other sugar-based candies, take care to do all of the following:

- Dissolve the sugar thoroughly by stirring the mixture well in the beginning.
- Always stir with a wooden spoon, not a metal one.
- Cook for the first few minutes with a cover on the saucepan to help dissolve sugar crystals and send them back into the mixture, or use a pastry brush to wash down the sides.
- Pour the syrup carefully from the saucepan to the cooling pan.
- Avoid making sugar-based candy on humid days.

Sugar Stages

Most candies are basically sugar cooked with liquid(s) and flavorings. As you heat the sugar mix, it goes through stages. These stages relate to the temperature of the sugar mix, which in turn relates to the concentration of sugar in the mix, which in turn determines the type of candy you get. Each stage has a name based on the characteristic ways the sugar mixture behaves when a bit of the mix is dropped into cold water.

To determine what stage your sugar mixture is at, drip a bit of the sugar syrup into cold water and test it with your fingers. **Caution**! Be careful not to burn yourself. Give the mixture time to cool in the water before you test it with your fingers. At the

- **Thread stage**, the syrup forms a liquid thread.
- **Soft-ball stage**, the syrup forms a soft ball. If you remove it from the water and place the ball on a small plate, the ball flattens.
- **Firm-ball stage**, the syrup forms a firm ball that stays together well but still has a bit of give when you squeeze it (very gently!). It won't flatten when placed on a small plate.
- **Hard-ball stage**, the syrup forms a hard ball that holds its shape on a plate. You can squish it flat, though.
- **Soft-crack stage**, the syrup forms threads that are flexible when removed from the water. They'll bend before breaking.
- **Hard-crack stage**, the syrup forms hard, brittle threads that break when you try to bend them.

I've updated my recipes with both the sugar stage and the temperature.

Sugar stages and temperatures

Stage	Example	Fahrenheit (°F)	Celsius (°C)
Thread	Syrup	230 to 234	110 to 112
Soft ball	Fudge, fondant	235 to 241	112 to 116
Firm ball	Caramels	244 to 248	118 to 120
Hard ball	Taffy	250 to 266	121 to 130
Soft crack	Saltwater taffy	270 to 289	132 to 143
Hard crack	Nut brittles	295 to 309	146 to 154
Clear liquid	NA	320	160
Brown liquid	Caramelized sugar	338	170
Burnt sugar	Burnt sugar	350	177

For greatest precision and certainty when making candy, I recommend getting a candy thermometer. Otherwise, it can be a nervous guessing game of whether the sugar is at the soft ball stage or at the firm ball stage—and that makes the difference between one kind of candy and another. Once the sugar mixture moves to the next stage, there's no going back.

My favorite thermometer is the ChefAlarm from ThermoWorks.com. The ChefAlarm has high and low alarms to alert you when your candy reaches the right stage of cooking and cooling, and you can use it for many other foods as well. Plus it comes in several different colors—bonus! Please buy directly from ThermoWorks; some people on Amazon sell inferior knockoffs.

Candy Molds Aren't All the Same

Candy molds come in many delightful shapes. But be aware that molds suitable for molding cooler candies, such as chocolate, may not be suitable for candies that are much hotter when poured into the mold, such as the Maple Syrup Candy (page 55).

If you don't have candy molds, or you're not certain you have the right kind for a recipe, you can use metal mini muffin tins for molding both chocolate and hotter candies.

Almond Paste

Prep/cook time: 10 minutes   Makes 14 ounces

Almond paste is expensive to buy, but super easy to make. An interesting cultural note: the terms "almond paste" and "marzipan" are used interchangeably in other countries, but in the United States, they're different products. Almond paste is equal amounts of almond meal and sugar; marzipan has much more sugar than it has almond meal. Although almond paste is not a candy, it's the basis for making Marzipan (page 56), which *is* considered a candy, so I'm including this recipe in this chapter. You also need this recipe for the delicious (and gluten-free!) Almond Crescents on page 65. If you're concerned about food safety, use pasteurized egg whites.

1½ cups finely ground
   blanched almond flour
1½ cups powdered sugar
⅛ teaspoon salt
1 large egg white

1 teaspoon almond extract
1 teaspoon rose water or
   orange blossom water
   (optional)

1   Combine the almond meal with the sugar and salt and mix well. A food processor makes this job a lot easier.
2   Add the remaining ingredients and work into a stiff, smooth paste.
3   Use immediately or store in refrigerator, tightly wrapped, for up to one month. You can also freeze it for up to three months. Bring to room temperature before using.

Chocolate Peanut Butter Bites

Prep/cook time: 10 minutes plus 2 hours to cool

Makes 2 dozen minis

Wanting something easy to make that tasted like peanut butter and chocolate, I invented this recipe many decades ago. I used to drop the mixture by tablespoons on a silicone mat, but later discovered the ease of using a mini muffin tin. I then made the further discovery of how greasing the tins with coconut oil not only makes it easier to unmold the chocolates, it also adds a delightful coconut flavor. You can use any type of chocolate chips you want, from milk to dark chocolate. The recipe works best if you use plain peanut butter with nothing added. Also, a health tip: it's best to buy only organic peanut butter.

¼ cup coconut oil
2 cups smooth peanut butter

2 cups chocolate chips

1 Lightly but thoroughly grease a 24-cup mini muffin tin with coconut oil. (A muffin tin with 24 wells, not the capacity to hold 24 cups of batter.)
2 Combine the peanut butter and chocolate in a medium sauce pan and heat over low to medium heat until the chocolate chips are melted and the peanut butter and chocolate are well combined. Be careful not to burn the chocolate chips.
3 Pour into the prepared mini muffin tin.
4 Cool in the refrigerator or freezer until firm.
5 Using the edge of a butter knife, gently pop each chocolate out of the tin.
6 Store in an airtight container in the refrigerator. Keeps for up to a month.

Cream Cheese Butter Mints

Prep/cook time: 2½ hours   Makes about four dozen

I love butter mints. Those tiny little pillows melt in your mouth with just a hint of sweetness and peppermint, and then they're gone. Turns out they are quite easy to make. I amalgamated several recipes to come up with this one.

4 ounces cream cheese, softened
1 tablespoon unsalted butter, softened

1 teaspoon peppermint extract
3 cups powdered sugar
Food coloring (optional, if you want to color your mints)

1   Combine all ingredients except the food coloring and mix well.
2   Optional step: if you want to color your mints, either delicately color the entire batch with one color, or divide the dough into portions, one for each color you want. For example, if you want pink, green, and yellow mints, divide the dough into three portions and color each.
3   Roll the dough into a long, tiny rope (about ½ inch in diameter).
4   Shape as desired:

- Using kitchen shears, snip into small pieces (about ½ inch long).
- Roll tiny bits of the dough into balls and flatten with a fork to make a pretty little cross-hatch pattern.

5   Place the individual candies on waxed paper or a silicone mat.
6   Dry at room temperature for two hours, then refrigerate. Keep refrigerated.

Creamy Dream Fudge

Prep/cook time: 1 hour 15 minutes   Makes one 13" x 9" panful

V ery easy, very smooth. This classic recipe is great for when you want fudge right now! And it's easy! You don't have to worry about sugar stages. Walnuts, almonds, or pecans are perfect in this recipe.

1 cup unsalted butter
3/4 cup cocoa powder
1 cup evaporated milk
2 pounds (7½ cups) powdered
    sugar

½ teaspoon kosher salt
2 teaspoons vanilla extract
1 cup chopped nuts
1 cup marshmallows (optional)

1   Thoroughly butter a 13" x 9" pan.
2   Melt butter in a large saucepan.
3   Add cocoa and blend well.
4   Stir in evaporated milk.
5   Gradually mix in sugar and salt until smooth and creamy.
6   Add vanilla and nuts. Stir until well blended.
7   Pour into pan and spread evenly.
8   Refrigerate until cool and firm (about 1 hour), or freeze for 20
     minutes, then cut into squares.

Devine's Peanut Butter Fudge

Prep/cook time: 35 minutes   Makes one 9" square pan

Mr. John Devine, a Court Clerk and former stock car racer in Tucson, Arizona, was kind enough to share this delicious recipe in the 1980s. I love the surprising touch of cocoa. His note for this recipe was "1 trillion calories minimum."

3 cups granulated sugar
2/3 cup cocoa powder
1 tablespoon salt
1½ cups whole milk

1 tablespoon vanilla extract
¼ cup unsalted butter, cut up
1 to 2 cups peanut butter

1   Butter a 9" x 9" glass pan.
2   Mix sugar, cocoa, and salt.
3   Add milk and mix thoroughly.
4   Put on medium heat and bring to soft ball stage (235° to 240° on a candy thermometer), stirring regularly. **Do not touch sides of pan with spoon while cooking.**
5   At the soft ball stage, stir in the butter. The mixture will start to thicken.
6   When the mixture starts to thicken, remove from heat and add vanilla and peanut butter. Mix quickly, then swiftly pour into buttered pan. Cut into pieces immediately. As Mr. Devine said in his original recipe, "Eat yummies from pan and spoon."

Honeycomb Candy

Prep/cook time: ten minutes, plus 3 hours cooling time

Makes 1 pound

I have fond memories of my mother buying this candy for my brothers and me in Sunnyvale, California. Also known as sea foam candy, sponge candy, cinder toffee, and hokey pokey, this recipe makes a feather-light, crunchy candy. It's best to entirely coat the pieces with chocolate, because this candy readily absorbs moisture from the air and, uncoated, becomes unpleasantly sticky. I adapted this recipe from ThoughtCo.com. Note that the flavor of the honey strongly affects the taste, so choose a honey whose flavor you like. **Important**! Have everything ready before you start this recipe.

½ cup honey
1¼ cups sugar (granulated or brown; you can also use superfine sugar)

1 pinch Himalayan pink sea salt
1 tablespoon baking soda
12 ounces of milk or dark chocolate (for coating)

1   Line a large baking sheet with a silicone baking mat (or butter the pan very well).
2   Place the honey, sugar, and salt in a large, deep stock pot. You can stir, but you don't need to. (You will think you don't need a large stock pot until you add the baking soda.)
3   Turn heat to high and bring to a boil **without stirring**. Continue boiling until it just reaches the hard crack stage (295°; about 5 minutes). **When it reaches 295°, immediately remove from heat.**
4   Quickly add the baking soda and whisk a few times. The candy will foam up. A lot. **Warning: it is very hot. Be careful and safe.**
5   Pour immediately onto the lined baking sheet. Don't spread it out or you'll pop the bubbles. It will look like a large chunk of foam; it will flatten as it cools. *Cleaning tip:* set the stock pot aside, fill with water, toss in the utensils, and let sit for an hour or so before you try washing up.
6   Cool the candy for about three hours or until it hardens.
7   Once it is completely cool and hard, break the candy into chunks.
8   Melt the chocolate and completely coat the pieces of honeycomb. Place the pieces, separate from each other, on a rack or the lined baking sheet to cool.

Maple Syrup Fudge

Prep/cook time: 1½ hours   Makes one 8" square pan

I found this delicious fudge recipe, which is similar to maple sugar candy, on the website VermontMaple.org. In the laconic New England way, the recipe didn't offer much in the way of instructions, so after cooking it a few times, I filled in the blanks. Note that this recipe uses pure maple syrup, not "maple flavored" pancake syrup, which is mostly sugar syrup with maple flavoring or a tiny amount of real maple syrup. Those syrups are inexpensive alternatives to maple syrup for your pancakes, but they won't work in this recipe because of cooking chemistry. Store the fudge tightly wrapped or in an airtight container.

2 cups pure maple syrup   **½** cup toasted chopped
⅓ cup heavy cream   walnuts (optional)

1   Prepare an 8" x 8" baking pan by buttering the bottoms and sides generously. If you are using nuts, sprinkle them in the pan. Set the pan aside.
2   Combine the maple syrup and cream in a very deep saucepan or stockpot. (As it cooks, it will rise pretty high.)
3   Bring to a boil on medium heat, stirring often, to the soft ball stage (238°—about 20 minutes). Remove from heat.
4   Cool until it is 150°. This takes half an hour, maybe more, maybe less, depending on room temperature. Check the fudge's temperature and stir regularly so that you don't have the problem of part of the fudge getting too cold while other parts stay too hot. If that happens, the fudge will freeze up when you beat it. Not a disaster, but you'll have to rescue it.
5   When the fudge reaches 150°, stir until it's a lighter color and thickened. I used my Kitchenaid stand mixer for this part, but you can do it by hand. It takes three to ten minutes depending on how cool the fudge is when you start.
6   Pour the fudge into the buttered pan. Let cool, then cut into pieces and enjoy.

Maple Syrup Candy

Prep/cook time: 25 minutes   Makes a varying amount (depends on
                                                                    mold size)

A soft candy made from pure maple syrup and nothing else, this is one of my favorites. If needed, you can cut the recipe in half. Flexible candy molds work best. The classic mold is a maple leaf, but you can use any shape you want. In a pinch, you can use mini muffin tins or a 13" x 9" baking pan.

1 quart pure maple syrup

1   Prepare molds or pans by very lightly greasing them with butter or cooking spray.
2   In a large saucepan, heat the maple syrup, stirring occasionally, to the soft ball stage (235° to 240°).
3   Remove from heat and cool to 175° **without stirring**. The cooling time should only be a few minutes, so hover nearby. If you're nervous, you can start stirring a bit before it reaches 175°.
4   When it reaches 175°, begin stirring. Stir constantly a few more minutes, or until the color is slightly lighter and the candy barely begins to stiffen. **Stop stirring when it reaches that stage.**
5   Quickly pour the syrup into molds to harden.
6   Remove from molds when cool.

Marzipan

Prep/cook time: 15 minutes   Makes about 2 pounds

In the US, marzipan is sweetened almond paste, sometimes with a few additional ingredients. (See page 48 for an almond paste recipe.) Marzipan is often dyed and shaped into fruits, flowers, animals, and other figures. If you're concerned about food safety, use pasteurized egg whites. For helpful, detailed instructions on things to do with marzipan, see Roland Mesnier's *Dessert University: More Than 300 Spectacular Recipes and Essential Lessons from White House Pastry Chef Roland Mesnier* (Simon & Schuster, 2004).

2 large egg whites   **14** ounces almond paste
2 teaspoons vanilla extract   **3** cups powdered sugar
1 teaspoon almond extract

1   Combine the egg whites with the vanilla and almond extract.
2   Knead the almond paste until it is soft, then use your hands
    to mix in the egg whites/extract mixture until well combined.
    (You can also use a food processor; if you do, use the paddle
    attachment.)
3   Add the powdered sugar 1 cup at a time, kneading the dough
    until the sugar is fully incorporated before adding the next cup.
    Keep kneading until the marzipan is smooth and pliable.
4   **If using immediately**, shape on silicone baking liners or on a
    board dusted with cornstarch or arrowroot powder. You might
    be tempted to dust the board with powdered sugar. Don't. The
    marzipan could become too dry. **If not using immediately**, wrap
    tightly in plastic wrap and refrigerate. Bring to room temperature
    before using.

Menuhune Butter

Prep/cook time: 10 minutes   Makes 4 pounds

When my former husband and I were honeymooning on the island of Kauai, we found a chocolate shop that served this delicious fudge they called Menehune Butter. You may have seen it as Tiger Fudge or Tiger Butter. This candy is so light it seems to melt in your mouth, leaving no touch but a lingering sense of the delightful and unfamiliar, like the Menuhune themselves. The Menuhune people were small in stature but large in legend: with no evidence for them aside from the impressive stone works they're credited with building, they were assumed to be a Hawaiian myth. The 2004 discoveries in Indonesia of humanoid skeletons only 1 meter tall (3.3 feet) lend credence to the legends.

3 pounds white chocolate, melted

1 pound crunchy peanut butter

8 to 12 ounces dark chocolate, melted

1   Mix white chocolate with the peanut butter.
2   Pour the white chocolate/peanut butter mix into shallow baking trays (to a depth of about a half inch or less).
3   Quickly swirl the melted semi-sweet chocolate into the top.
4   Cool.

Mrs. Paxton's Almond Toffee

Prep/cook time: 2 hours   Makes one 13" x 9" pan

Mrs. Paxton, the Virginian mother of my high school sweetheart, was a wonderfully funny woman. She would sneak to his bedroom when he and I grew unusually quiet, only to find us each absorbed in reading science fiction, rather than each other as she'd expected. She'd shake her head and say, "Those durn kids." Mrs. Paxton, wherever you are, thanks for everything—including this recipe.

1 pound unsalted butter
1 pound packed brown sugar

2⅔ cups semisweet chocolate chips
½ cup finely chopped, toasted almonds

1   Depending on how thick you want your toffee, choose a 13" x 9" pan up to a 15½" x 10½" baking sheet. Prepare the pan by buttering it very, very well. Then sprinkle it generously with the almonds.
2   Mix the butter and sugar together and heat, stirring constantly, to the hard ball stage (250° to 265°). Watch it like a hawk—it can burn in an instant.
3   As soon as the candy reaches the hard ball stage, pour it over the almonds on the prepared pan. Let it cool and harden.
4   When the toffee is cool and hard, melt half of the chocolate chips and spread over the top of the toffee. Let harden at least 1 hour. (Or 20 minutes in the freezer.)
5   Carefully flip the entire piece of toffee (this is the hardest part of the recipe: prying that toffee out of its lodgings and flipping it without breaking it into smithereens.) You may be forced to break off a piece and taste it in order to create a toehold for your knife (or whatever implement you're using to pry the toffee).
6   Melt the remainder of the chocolate and spread over the newly exposed side of the candy. Let harden. Break into pieces and enjoy.

Peppermint Patties

Prep/cook time: about 1 hour   Makes about 36 wafers

I love peppermint, and I love peppermint patties. It's so easy (though a bit messy) to make your own. And fast! And inexpensive! You'll find a lot of variations of this recipe online, but many call for corn syrup (which I prefer not to use). I tried several recipes and ended up slightly modifying this one from the OhNuts.com blog. These patties freeze well.

2½ cups powdered sugar
2 tablespoons unsalted butter, softened

2 teaspoons peppermint extract
2 tablespoons heavy cream
2 cups dark chocolate chips

1   Combine powdered sugar, butter, peppermint extract, and cream in a medium bowl. Beat gently until everything comes together and the candy dough is stiff. If it's too wet, add more powdered sugar a little at a time.
2   Put the candy dough on a long piece of cling wrap and form into a tube about 1½ to 2 inches in diameter. Wrap the candy dough well with cling wrap. Don't leave any exposed to air (because it dries out quickly). Optionally, you can slice a cardboard paper towel tube lengthwise and put the wrapped candy dough inside. This helps keep it round as it chills.
3   Chill in the refrigerator or freezer for about an hour. Some people say never freeze the candy dough, others say always freeze it. I've tried it both ways and find that freezing works better than fridging to keep the candy from melting when you're dipping it.
4   Melt the chocolate chips and place in a small container.
5   Remove the candy dough from the refrigerator or freezer. Unwrap and slice into ¼ inch slices. From here you'll need to work quickly, as it's best to dip while the candy dough is still cold.
6   Use a fork or candy dipping tool to dip one patty at a time into the melted chocolate. Coat completely. If you leave it in too long, the patty will melt.
7   Place each dipped wafer onto a silicone mat or a cooling rack.
8   Cool completely, then store in an airtight container. If the weather is hot, keep in the refrigerator.

Rocky Road Fudge

Prep/cook time: 2 hours 20 minutes   Makes 5 pounds

This easy recipe makes a lot of richly flavored fudge. It's a good choice for holiday gift giving. Use one 13" x 9" and one 9" x 9" pan, or one jelly roll pan (15" x 10" x 1"), though a jelly roll pan makes slightly thinner pieces.

$4\frac{1}{2}$ cups granulated sugar
1 can evaporated milk
3 cups chocolate chips
1 cup unsalted butter, cut up

2 cups chopped nuts
2 tablespoons vanilla extract
10 ounces miniature
  marshmallows

1   Prepare pans by buttering them well.
2   Mix the sugar and milk well in a large saucepan. Bring to a full boil and boil ten minutes. Remove from heat.
3   Add the remaining ingredients to the sugar/milk mixture. Pour quickly into buttered pans.
4   Cover with plastic wrap and cool 2 hours in refrigerator.

Soldier's Fudge

Prep/cook time: 1 hour 15 minutes   Makes 2 pounds

As near as I can tell, variations of this recipe have been kicking around for close to a century (or possibly longer) under different names. I first saw it in the early 1970s, and it had already been around a while then. This fudge has many virtues, among them the speed with which you can make it (about 20 minutes to make it, plus chilling time), and the remarkable tastiness that you achieve without having to worry about sugar stages. This is my favorite variation copied out of a long-lost cookbook.

14 ounces sweetened condensed milk	**1** ounce unsweetened chocolate
2 cups semisweet chocolate chips	**1** teaspoon vanilla extract
	1½ cups chopped nuts

1   Butter an 8" x 8" baking pan.
2   Heat milk, chocolate chips, and unsweetened chocolate in a 2-quart saucepan over low heat, stirring constantly, until chocolate is melted and mixture is smooth (about 15 minutes).
3   Remove from heat and stir in vanilla and nuts.
4   Spread mixture evenly in pan.
5   Refrigerate until firm (about 1 hour). Cut into 1-inch squares.

Vinegar Taffy

Prep/cook time: 2 hours   Makes about 72 pieces

My brothers and I often made this candy when we were children. Although the name says "taffy," this is a hard candy, not soft like a saltwater taffy. It's buttery and smooth; well worth the effort!

2 tablespoons butter   2 cups granulated sugar
½ cup water   1 teaspoon vanilla extract
2 tablespoons vinegar

1   Lightly butter a shallow pan or platter.
2   Melt the butter in a 2-quart saucepan. Roll it around the sides of the pan to grease the saucepan well.
3   Add water and vinegar to the pan and bring to a boil.
4   When the water mixture is boiling, carefully stir in the sugar so that it is completely dissolved. Try not to get any sugar crystals on the sides of the pan.
5   Cover saucepan and cook for 3 to 5 minutes or until any sugar crystals that you may have inadvertently gotten on the sides are melted down from the sides of the pan.
6   Uncover pan and continue rapidly boiling the syrup to the hard ball stage (262°).
7   Remove from heat. Holding the saucepan an inch or so above the surface, carefully pour into the prepared pan or platter to the depth of about ½ inch. **Do not scrape the last of the syrup from the pan**.
8   Sprinkle with vanilla, but don't stir it in.
9   Let the candy cool undisturbed until it can be held comfortably in the hands.
10 Once the candy is cool enough, knead it gently until you can pull and fold it. If the candy has been cooked correctly, it shouldn't stick to your hands (though you may want to butter your hands). Pull taffy into ropes, then fold and pull again. Keep pulling and folding until it has a satin-like finish and breaks off when hit against a hard surface. At that point, pull into ropes of desired thickness and cut into inch-long lengths with buttered scissors..

Cookies

The world's vast variety of cookie recipes is a testament to our love of the tasty little bites. We call them different things in different regions of the world, but whatever we call them—biscuits, biscotti, cookies, or even crackers—we humans enjoy making, sharing, and eating cookies.

Cookie shapes, ingredients, and methods vary wildly. Cookies can be baked on sheets and then cut up (bar cookies); rolled into balls; dropped by spoonfuls on a baking sheet; rolled out like pie crust and cut into shapes; pressed into molds (such as with shortbread); or formed into logs and refrigerated, then sliced. Their primary characteristic is that we can hold one in our hands to eat it.

I've included my favorite cookie recipes in this chapter, from family favorites handed down through several generations (see Abernethy Biscuits on page 64 and Snow-Covered Gingersnaps on page 86) to new favorites. Maybe you'll recognize some of your own family treasures, or discover some new ones.

Note: According to Stef Pollack of the CupcakeProject.com, when making cookies, you can substitute mayonnaise for eggs at a ratio of 3 tablespoons mayonnaise for each egg with good results. I haven't tried this yet myself, so I can't say from personal experience, but Ms. Pollak seems to know her stuff and to have tested this thoroughly.

Abernethy Biscuits

Prep/cook time: 30 minutes   Makes about 4 dozen

This favorite recipe has been in my family for several generations. Long ago, my mother gave me her only copy (she, of course, had it memorized). Then I lost it, and she was no longer around to ask. I was unhappy with myself. How could I be so careless? When the Internet became a thing, I searched for and found Abernethy Biscuit recipes, but none were the same as our family's recipe. Fortunately, after many years, I found the family version again. These are called biscuits because they come from England. What we Americans call cookies, the British call biscuits. John Abernethy, a London-born doctor in the 1700s, promoted these as an aid to digestion. Serve warm or cool with fresh hot tea.

1 cup unsalted butter
1 cup granulated sugar
1 teaspoon vanilla extract
1 large egg, beaten well

1 cup sour cream
3¾ cups all-purpose flour
1 teaspoon baking soda
2 teaspoons caraway seeds

1   Preheat oven to 425°.
2   Cream butter, sugar, and vanilla together.
3   Add the egg and sour cream and mix well, then add flour, baking soda, and caraway seeds and mix thoroughly. The dough should be silky and not very sticky.
4   Roll dough out to about ¾ inch thick. (For crisper cookies, roll thinner.)
5   Cut into 2-inch rounds.
6   Place on an ungreased baking sheet and bake about 12 minutes or until a very pale tan in color.

Almond Crescents

Prep/cook time: 50 minutes   Makes about 16 crescents

T rader Joe's, a California-based chain of grocery stores with a unique personality, carried almond horn cookies for a few years, then stopped. I loved them in part because I love almonds, and in part because they're gluten free. I later found it's a classic German recipe called Mandelhörnchen (little almond horns). This slight adaptation of Kimberly Killebrew's recipe (DaringGourmet.com) makes cookies that are even better than Trader Joe's. **For this recipe, you must use almond paste, not marzipan**. You can use store-bought almond paste, but why not make your own? See page 48 for an almond paste recipe.

8 ounces almond paste
1 cup finely ground blanched almond flour
1 cup powdered sugar
½ teaspoon almond extract

2 teaspoons fresh lemon juice
2 large egg whites, divided
1 cup sliced almonds
1⅓ cups chocolate chips

1   Combine the almond paste with the almond meal, powdered sugar, almond extract, lemon juice, and one of the egg whites.
2   Knead the mixture until it comes together. It's okay if it's a bit sticky. Add more almond flour if it's too sticky.
3   Wrap the dough in plastic wrap and chill 30 minutes. (More chill time is okay; you can even make the dough a few days ahead.)
4   Preheat the oven to 325°.
5   Break the dough into pieces and roll each piece into a 1-inch ball. Roll each ball into a small log (about 3 inches long), tapering it at each end. Bend each into a crescent shape, like crescent moons.
6   Brush each cookie on all sides with the second egg white, then coat each cookie on all sides with the sliced almonds.
7   Place cookies on a lined baking sheet. The cookies puff up a bit while baking, so give them some room.
8   Bake 10-15 minutes or until the tips just start to turn golden.
9   Remove from oven and cool completely.
10 Melt the chocolate chips. Dip each end of the crescents, then the bottoms, into the chocolate. Place each dipped cookie onto a lined baking sheet with the chocolate side up. Cool until the chocolate hardens.

Almond Macaroons

Prep/cook time: 1 hour   Makes about 2½ dozen

Historically and in other countries, macaroons were and are made with almond flour, though you'll find plenty of variations. Many macaroon recipes use almond paste and are similar to the Almond Crescents on page 65. In the US, the most common macaroon heavily features shredded coconut shaped into a cute little haystack. I love coconut macaroons, especially when they've been dipped in chocolate (an option with this recipe if you like). In this recipe, unlike with standard macaroons, the only contribution from almonds is in the form of chopped almonds and almond extract.

2⅔ cups flaked unsweetened coconut
⅔ cup granulated sugar
¼ cup all-purpose flour
¼ teaspoon salt

4 large egg whites, room temperature
1 teaspoon almond extract
1 cup chopped almonds

1   Combine the coconut, sugar, flour, and salt in a mixing bowl.
2   Beat the egg whites until they make medium-firm peaks.
3   Carefully fold the egg whites into the coconut mixture.
4   Add the almond extract. Mix well.
5   Stir in the almonds.
6   Drop batter by the teaspoon onto lightly greased baking sheets or baking sheets lined with silicone mats.
7   Bake at 325° for 20 to 25 minutes, or until edges are golden brown. Remove from baking sheets immediately.

Brandied Ginger Balls

Prep/cook time: 45 minutes Makes 2 dozen

This traditional holiday cookie keeps well and is a nice addition to a gift basket. Many recipes for brandied ginger balls are no-bake and involve crushing gingersnaps or other cookies to make the base. This recipes requires baking and doesn't require having cookies on hand to crush. Nothing against the no-bake versions—they're delicious too!—just this is the one I've been making for years.

1 cup unsalted butter, softened	1½ teaspoons ground ginger
½ cup packed brown sugar	½ teaspoon freshly grated
½ cup molasses	nutmeg
2 tablespoons brandy or dry sherry	½ teaspoon salt
2 cups all-purpose flour	½ cup powdered sugar

1   Preheat oven to 300°. Grease or line a baking sheet.
2   Cream together the butter, brown sugar, molasses, and brandy.
3   Add flour, ginger, nutmeg, and salt to butter mixture. Mix well.
4   Form into 1-inch balls.
5   Place balls on baking sheets and bake 15 minutes.
6   After baking, immediately remove to a platter and sift powdered sugar over them while still warm.

Brownie Pie

Prep/cook time: 1 hour   Makes one 9" pie

Brownies are said to have made their debut at the Chicago World's Fair in 1893. The original recipe called for a pound each of chocolate and butter. This recipe isn't really a pie—just a deliciously chewy, dark chocolate brownie baked in a pie pan. Cut into pie-shaped slices and serve warm with ice cream or whipped cream. For the s'mores variation, you can use any size marshmallow from mini to maxi.

½ cup unsalted butter
2 ounces unsweetened
   chocolate
1 cup granulated sugar
¾ cup all-purpose flour

2 large eggs, lightly beaten
½ teaspoon baking powder
½ teaspoon salt
1 teaspoon vanilla extract

1   Preheat oven to 350°. Butter a 9" pie pan.
2   Put butter and unsweetened chocolate in a 2-quart saucepan. Heat, stirring occasionally, over medium heat until melted (about 5 minutes).
3   Stir in sugar, flour, eggs, baking powder, salt, and vanilla.
4   Spread batter in pie pan and bake for 20 to 25 minutes or until brownie is firm to the touch.
5   Remove brownie pie from oven. Cool 30 minutes if you can stand to wait that long.

Brownie Pie Peanut Butter S'Mores Variation

1 recipe brownie pie
¾ cup peanut butter

1½ cups marshmallows

1   Bake the brownie pie as above.
2   As soon as you take the pan out of the oven, spread with peanut butter and top with a single layer of marshmallows.
3   Return to the oven and bake a few more minutes, or until the marshmallows are puffy and golden.

Brownies

Prep/cook time: 1 hour   Makes one 13" x 9" pan

T hese brownies are moist, slightly fudgy, and not too sweet. The difference between fudgy brownies and cake-like brownies is in the ratio of fat to flour. The
higher the ratio of fat to flour, the fudgier the brownies. The higher the ratio of flour
to fat, the more cake-like the brownies will be. Because chocolate has more fat in it
than cocoa, fudgier brownies often use chocolate, and cake-like brownies often use
cocoa. Most of my favorite recipes are on the fudgy side.

6 ounces unsweetened
chocolate
¾ cup unsalted butter
4 large eggs
2 tablespoons vanilla extract
½ teaspoon salt

2 cups granulated sugar
1½ cups whole wheat pastry
flour
1½ cups chopped walnuts
1½ cups chocolate chips

1   Preheat oven to 375°.
2   Butter and lightly flour a 13" x 9" baking pan.
3   In a heavy-bottomed saucepan, melt the chocolate and butter
over low heat, watching and stirring often. When melted, remove
from heat and cool.
4   Combine the eggs, vanilla, salt, and sugar, and beat well (an
electric mixer is okay) for 8 to 10 minutes.
5   Gently stir in the chocolate, then add the flour, stirring only until
blended.
6   Stir in the walnuts and chocolate chips.
7   Spread batter evenly in pan and bake for 25 minutes. When done,
the center should be moist.
8   Remove from the oven and let cool slightly, then cut into squares
while still warm.

Caramel Crunch Bars

Prep/cook time: 1 hour   Makes one 13" x 9" pan

You bake these irresistible bars in two stages. For the caramel, you can use a commercial caramel topping, but I recommend trying your hand at making your own—it's very easy! Try the Caramel Sauce recipe on page 107.

1 cup plus 3 tablespoons all-purpose flour
1 cup oatmeal
3/4 cup packed brown sugar
1/2 teaspoon baking soda

1/4 teaspoon salt
1/2 cup unsalted butter, melted
2 cups chocolate chips
2 cups caramel sauce
1/2 cup chopped or whole nuts

1   Preheat oven to 350°.

Stage 1

2   Mix the 1 cup flour with the oatmeal, brown sugar, baking soda, and salt.
3   Place mixture in a 13" x 9" baking pan.
4   Bake for 10 minutes.
5   Remove from oven.

Stage 2

6   Sprinkle the base in the baking pan with the chocolate chips and nuts.
7   Mix the 3 tablespoons of flour with the caramel sauce.
8   Pour caramel mixture evenly over the chocolate chips and nuts.
9   Bake again for 20 to 25 minutes.

Chai-Spiced Tea Cookies

Prep/cook time: 40 minutes   Makes 2½ dozen

W hen made properly, these cookies are tender and a bit crumbly. You can store them in an airtight container for up to three days. (They don't keep long.) Experiment with types and quantities of tea leaves to discover your own favorite combinations. My daughter lightly adapted this recipe from Anissa Shea's runner-up entry in *Sunset* magazine's Holiday Cookie contest (December 2011).

1 cup unsalted butter, softened
½ cup granulated sugar
½ teaspoon salt
1 teaspoon vanilla extract
2 cups all-purpose flour
1 tablespoon ground cinnamon
1¼ teaspoons ground ginger

1 teaspoon fennel seeds, ground
½ teaspoon ground cardamom
2 teaspoons loose black tea, such as Darjeeling or Barry's Gold

1   Line two baking sheets with silicone baking mats or parchment paper. (Avoid aluminum foil; it will cook the bottom of the cookies too quickly.)
2   Preheat oven to 325°.
3   Combine butter, sugar, salt, and vanilla. Cream together until silky.
4   In another bowl, combine the flour, cinnamon, ginger, fennel, cardamom, and tea leaves.
5   Add the flour-spice mixture to the butter mixture and beat gently until the dough is silky.
6   Form into 1-inch balls and place on baking sheets 1 inch apart. Flatten slightly.
7   Bake 8 to 10 minutes. Halfway through baking, rotate the baking sheets. If baking multiple sheets at once, swap the baking sheets as well. Bake until cookies are a light golden brown on the bottom. This will be hard to tell because the dough is already brown.
8   Remove from oven and immediately (but gently!) remove from baking sheets. Cool cookies on racks.

Chocolate Chip Cookies

Prep/cook time: 1 hour   Makes 4 dozen

Everyone in America has their favorite "best" chocolate chip cookie recipe. They're all the best recipe. Here's our favorite. It started on the back of a Guittard chocolate chip package. Of course, we modified the recipe to suit our tastes—a little more of *this*, a little less of *that*, and, in our household, no nuts in the batter because my daughter doesn't like them. Sometimes I press walnut halves onto some of the cookies before baking.

2¼ cups all-purpose flour
1 teaspoon baking soda
½ teaspoon salt
1 cup unsalted butter, softened
½ cup granulated sugar

1 cup packed brown sugar
2 large eggs
4 teaspoons vanilla extract
3 cups chocolate chips

1   Combine flour with baking soda and salt; set aside.
2   In large mixing bowl, beat butter with vanilla and sugars.
3   Add eggs and mix gently until well blended.
4   Gradually stir flour mixture into butter-sugar mixture.
5   Stir in chocolate chips.
6   Using a tablespoon, drop onto baking sheets lined with silicone baking mats or parchment paper. (If you have neither, use ungreased baking sheets.)
7   Bake at 350° for 9 to 11 minutes or until golden brown.

Chocolate Chocolate Chip Cookies

Prep/cook time: 1 hour   Makes 3 dozen 3" cookies

In this chocolate chip cookie recipe, the batter is chocolate. These richly chocolate cookies are cooked low and slow to keep them tender.

1 cup unsalted butter
1 cup packed brown sugar
3/4 cup granulated sugar
2 teaspoons vanilla extract
3 large eggs
2 1/4 cups all-purpose flour

1/2 cup natural cocoa powder
1/4 teaspoon salt
1/2 teaspoon baking soda
2 cups semisweet chocolate chips
1 cup chopped pecans

1   Preheat oven to 300°.
2   Cream butter, sugars, and vanilla together in a large bowl.
3   Beat in the eggs.
4   Combine the flour, cocoa, salt, and baking soda in a separate bowl.
5   Gradually add flour mixture to the creamed mixture.
6   Stir in chocolate chips.
7   Drop rounded tablespoonfuls (about two measuring tablespoons) of dough 3 inches apart onto an ungreased baking sheet.
8   Bake for 25 minutes. Remove to cooling rack.

Chocolate Crackle Cookies

Prep/cook time: 3 hours (including   Makes 4 dozen
chilling time)

A classic holiday cookie, moist, tender, and richly chocolate. Unfortunately, these cookies go stale in just two days. So they aren't good for shipping to friends, but they're great for making to share with friends on the spot. There are many versions of this recipe; here, I adapted Martha Stewart's recipe.

8 ounces bittersweet chocolate, melted
1¼ cups all-purpose flour
½ cup Dutch process cocoa powder
2 teaspoons baking powder
¼ teaspoon salt

½ cup unsalted butter, softened
1⅓ cups packed brown sugar
1 teaspoon vanilla extract
2 large eggs
⅓ cup whole milk
1 cup powdered sugar

1 Preheat oven to 350°.
2 Combine flour, cocoa, baking powder, and salt and set aside.
3 Beat butter, brown sugar, and vanilla together until light and fluffy.
4 Add eggs to the butter mixture and beat until well combined.
5 While stirring, slowly drizzle cooled chocolate into the butter mix.
6 Alternately add dry ingredients and milk, starting and ending with milk, until just combined. Mix gently or on low speed.
7 Divide the dough into quarters, then wrap each quarter with plastic wrap. Chill 2 hours or until firm.
8 When the dough is chilled, roll each ball into a log 1 to 1½ inches in diameter. The dough will be sticky and hard to handle. Use cocoa powder to minimize sticking.
9 Wrap logs in plastic wrap, and chill for another 30 minutes.
10 Cut each log into half-inch slices. A few at a time, toss the slices into a bag with the powdered sugar. Make sure the slices are completely covered with sugar.
11 Place slices onto a lined baking sheet. These cookies will spread a little, so give them room.
12 Bake until the cookie tops split (about 12 minutes).
13 Remove from oven; transfer immediately to a wire rack to cool.

Cinnamon Cookies

Prep/cook time: 2 hours   Makes about 2½ dozen

T hese cookies are light, delicate, crispy on the edges and soft in the middle. Some people call them Snickerdoodles. Variations of this recipe date back to the American Revolution. I got this recipe in the 1970s from Pat Grimmer, a formidable Scrabble player. Her brother Mike and I attended Santa Clara University together.

Ingredients for the Cookies

1 cup salted butter
1½ cups granulated sugar
2 large eggs

2¾ cups all-purpose flour
2 teaspoons cream of tartar
1 teaspoon baking soda

Ingredients for the Topping

3 tablespoons granulated sugar

3 tablespoons ground cinnamon

1   Cream the butter and the 1½ cups sugar together.
2   Add the eggs, flour, cream of tartar, and baking soda, mixing well after each addition.
3   Chill for 1 hour or until firm.
4   After chilling, roll batter into 1-inch balls.
5   Combine topping ingredients and roll the chilled balls in this mixture.
6   Place balls, well-spaced, on a baking sheet and bake at 400° for 8 minutes. (As they cook, they flatten considerably.)
7   Remove from oven and place on cooling racks immediately. They'll be quite delicate at first; cool slightly, then dive in.

Lemon Bars

Prep/cook time: 1 hour   Makes one 13" x 9" pan

T his bar cookie has a shortbread crust topped with a tangy lemon custard. Melting the butter results in a flatter shortbread with a denser texture—not desirable in normal shortbread, but perfect for supporting the custard in this recipe.

Ingredients for the Shortbread Crust

2 cups all-purpose flour   **½** cup powdered sugar
1 cup salted butter, melted

Ingredients for the Lemon Custard

2 tablespoons all-purpose flour   **½** cup lemon juice, fresh
2 cups granulated sugar   **2 to 3** teaspoons fresh lemon
1 teaspoon baking powder   zest (zest of 1 lemon)
4 large eggs, lightly beaten

Making the Shortbread Crust

1   Combine the 2 cups of flour with the melted butter and the powdered sugar.
2   Press mixture into the bottom of a 13" x 9" glass baking pan.
3   Bake at 350° for 18 to 20 minutes.

Making the Lemon Custard

1   While the crust is cooking, combine the 2 tablespoons of flour with the sugar and baking powder.
2   Add eggs, lemon juice, and lemon zest to the sugar/flour/baking powder mix. Mix thoroughly.

Combining Crust and Custard

1   When the crust is done, remove from the oven and immediately pour the custard over it.
2   Reduce oven temperature to 325°.
3   Return pan to oven for 20 to 25 minutes. Cook until the custard is a pale golden brown and no longer runny. If the custard starts to brown too quickly, cover loosely with aluminum foil.
4   Remove from oven and sprinkle liberally with powdered sugar.
5   Cool, then cut into 1½-inch squares.

Louise's Scottish Shortbread

Prep/cook time: 1 hour 30 minutes   Makes 2½ dozen

My friend Louise Nicholson, her twin Jolie Mason (née Nicholson) and I used to get together on New Year's Eve to talk, make these cookies, and drink tea. Louise's children and my daughter would get their own chunk of dough to roll out and cut into shapes with cookie cutters. The brown sugar adds a lovely flavor to the shortbread. If you double the recipe, maintain correct proportions between the flour and butter (by weight, not volume). For a crisper shortbread, add moisture (which activates the gluten in the flour), such as 1 teaspoon vanilla extract or 1 tablespoon sour cream.

2 cups all-purpose flour   **1** cup unsalted butter, softened
¼ teaspoon salt   ½ cup packed brown sugar
¼ teaspoon baking powder

1 Combine flour, salt, and baking powder. Set aside.
2 Cream butter and sugar together.
3 Mix flour mixture in with the butter and sugar mixture. Use your hands to pull dough into a ball. It will be crumbly and a bit dry.
4 Roll out to ¼ inch thick (thicker if you want a tenderer cookie). Use cookie cutters to cut into interesting shapes, or use a traditional shortbread cookie roller or a shortbread baking dish sprayed with cooking spray and lightly dusted with powdered sugar.
5 Bake at 350° for 10 to 15 minutes or until delicately brown.
6 Remove from oven and cool on wire racks.

Norwegian Butter Cookies

Prep/cook time: 30 minutes   Makes about 2 dozen

My mother used to make these round balls of buttery goodness for the winter holidays. It's possible that this recipe came to her through one of her Norwegian in-laws (the Norskogs). Other countries have similar cookies. Greece has its *Kourabiedes*. Mexico has its Mexican Wedding Cakes. Russia has Russian Tea Cakes. They're all pretty much the same: hard, very pale, slightly crumbly, and entirely delicious cookies made with butter, sugar, flour, and finely chopped nuts. The keen-eyed among you may be wondering, and no, that's not a typo: you do indeed mix all the ingredients together at once, instead of creaming the butter and sugar as a separate step.

1 cup salted butter
1/2 cup powdered sugar plus
    more for dusting the
    cookies
2 teaspoons vanilla extract

2 cups all-purpose flour
3/4 cup finely chopped nuts
    (almonds, hazelnuts, pecans,
    or walnuts)

1   Combine butter, powdered sugar, vanilla, flour, and nuts. Mix until a fine consistency.

2   Form into 1-inch balls. Then choose how to bake them:

   •   **Choice A**: Roll the balls in powdered sugar, then bake on an ungreased baking sheet at 375° for 10 to 12 minutes.

   •   **Choice B**: Place the balls on an ungreased baking sheet and bake at 325° for 15 to 20 minutes. Remove from oven and dust the cookies with powdered sugar.

Parlies

Prep/cook time: 30 minutes   Makes 12 dozen

When researching my family tree, I found I have a number of Scottish ancestors. So I researched Scottish cookies, too (of course), and found this
recipe in an old book (this was pre-Internet days). According to that book, these
thin, flat, crisp cookies were popular with members of the Scottish parliament in old
Edinburgh, who bought them in a nearby bake shop. (Hence the name—Parlies for
parliament.) Some versions of this recipe include one egg. This is a good recipe for
children to make, as it is fairly forgiving.

1 cup unsalted butter, melted   **4** cups all-purpose flour
1 cup molasses   **4** teaspoons ground ginger
1 cup packed brown sugar

1   Combine the butter and molasses in a saucepan and bring to a
    boil, stirring constantly. Remove from heat.
2   Blend in the brown sugar.
3   Add the flour and ginger and mix thoroughly. The dough will be
    fairly stiff.
4   While the mixture is still hot, roll out the dough, a small amount
    at a time, on a lightly floured board. It should be quite thin—¼
    inch or so. Cut into 2-inch diamonds with a knife or metal cookie
    cutter (or use any shape you want), then put on a greased baking
    sheet.
5   Bake at 325° for 15 minutes, or until lightly browned.
6   Remove from oven and cool on wire racks.

Peanut Butter Squares

Prep/cook time: 10 minutes   Makes 12 small balls

Some people call these "no bake cookies"; others call them "snacks." I call them the delicious culmination of much experimentation in creating the easiest, tastiest, and most healthful peanut butter bars ever. You can also make them with almond butter. To make them dairy free, substitute rice milk powder for the nonfat milk powder. These instructions say to press the mix into a baking pan, but you can also roll them into 1-inch balls.

1 cup rolled oats
1½ cups peanut butter
½ cup unsweetened, shredded coconut
½ cup nonfat milk powder

¼ cup chocolate chips
¼ cup raisins or currants
⅓ cup pure maple syrup
1 teaspoon vanilla extract
⅛ teaspoon Himalayan salt

1   Line an 11" x 7" glass baking pan with plastic wrap.
2   Combine all ingredients in a medium bowl. Mix well.
3   Press the mix into the lined pan.
4   Refrigerate an hour, then cut into squares. Store in an airtight container. Keep refrigerated.

Peanut Butter Cookies

Prep/cook time: 22 minutes   Makes 1 dozen

Thisremarkably easy recipe requires no flour, so it's good for those who are avoiding wheat or gluten. This recipe works best with peanut butter that's just peanuts and salt. You can also use almond butter instead of peanut butter. The results are cookies that are fragile but thoroughly delicious. The cookies are quite delicate when you first remove them from the oven, but they firm up as they cool. Consider tossing in some chocolate chips.

1 cup peanut butter (plain or crunchy)

1 cup granulated sugar
1 large egg

1   Line a baking sheet with parchment paper or a silicone mat.
2   Combine all ingredients. The mixture should barely hold together.
3   Drop by tablespoonsful onto the baking sheet.
4   Use a fork to flatten and make a cross-hatch pattern on each cookie.
5   Bake at 350° for 10 to 12 minutes. The cookies will be very crumbly at first, though they will hold together better when they cool.

Pretzel Peanut Butter Bars

Prep/cook time: 1½ hours   Makes enough to fill one 11" x 7" pan

My friends Chris and his aunt shared this recipe with me years ago. For a delicious gluten-free version, use Snyder's of Hanover's gluten-free pretzel sticks. The cast iron skillet is my suggestion; you can use any method you want to melt the butter and the chocolate-peanut butter mix.

¾ cup unsalted butter
2 cups crushed pretzel sticks
1 cup powdered sugar

1 cup plus ¼ cup peanut butter
1½ cups semisweet chocolate
   chips

1   Very lightly butter an 11" x 7" pan. (For thinner bars, use a 13" x 9" pan.)
2   Melt the butter in a cast iron skillet.
3   In a medium bowl, combine the melted butter, crushed pretzels, powdered sugar, and 1 cup of the peanut butter. Mix well.
4   Press the mixture into the buttered pan.
5   In the same iron skillet you melted the butter in, combine the chocolate chips and the remaining peanut butter. Heat over medium-low heat, stirring frequently, until the chocolate chips are completely melted and blended with the peanut butter.
6   Pour the chocolate over the pretzel mix in a thin, even layer.
7   Refrigerate one hour, then cut into small squares.

Pumpkin Cookies

Prep/cook time: 1 hour 30 minutes   Makes 6 dozen

n excellent, cake-like, moist cookie, perfect for fall and winter.

½ cup unsalted butter, softened	1 teaspoon baking powder
1½ cups granulated sugar	1 teaspoon baking soda
1 large egg	½ teaspoon salt
1 cup pumpkin purée	1 teaspoon ground nutmeg
1 teaspoon vanilla extract	1 teaspoon ground cinnamon
2½ cups all-purpose flour	½ cup almonds
	1 cup chocolate chips

1 Cream butter and sugar until light and fluffy.
2 Beat in egg, pumpkin, and vanilla.
3 In a separate bowl, combine the flour, baking powder, baking soda, salt, nutmeg, and cinnamon.
4 Add dry mix to the wet batter; mix well.
5 Add nuts and chocolate chips. Mix thoroughly.
6 Drop by the teaspoon onto well-greased baking sheets.
7 Bake at 350° for 15 minutes or until lightly browned.
8 Remove from baking sheet and cool on wire racks.

Rum Balls

Prep/cook time: 1 hour   Makes 4 dozen balls

Another holiday classic; this one requires no cooking. I use Famous brand chocolate wafers. If you like coffee, you can add 1½ tablespoons instant coffee powder with the sugar and walnuts.

8 ounces chocolate cookie wafers
1½ cups plus ½ cup powdered sugar

1¼ cups finely chopped walnuts
¼ teaspoon cream of tartar
⅓ to ½ cup rum

1   Crush cookies into fine crumbs (you should have about two cups of crumbs).
2   Add the 1½ cups of the sugar and the walnuts. Mix thoroughly.
3   Add cream of tartar.
4   Gradually stir in enough rum to form a stiff dough.
5   Roll into 1-inch balls, then roll balls in the remaining powdered sugar.
6   Store loosely packed between sheets of waxed paper or foil in an airtight container for up to two weeks.

Seven-Layer Bars

Prep/cook time: 1 hour 30 minutes   Makes one 13" x 9" pan

T hese cookies meet with approval everywhere I've taken them. Once baked, these cookies freeze well. Here's an interesting side note: When I first made these back in the early 1980s, a package of graham crackers (not the box, but the individual package inside the box) held 15 crackers. Now it holds 9.

½ cup unsalted butter, melted
2 cups graham cracker crumbs
1 can (14 ounces) sweetened
   condensed milk
1½ cups semisweet chocolate
   chips

½ cup butterscotch chips
½ cup white chocolate chips
½ cup flaked coconut
   (sweetened or
   unsweetened)
1 cup pecan halves

1 Pour melted butter into a 13" x 9" pan.
2 Sprinkle pan with the graham cracker crumbs and mix in the butter. Pressing firmly, shape the bottom and sides. You don't need to go all the way up—just form a small ½ inch rim.
3 Pour the sweetened condensed milk over the crumbs.
4 Scatter the chocolate chips, butterscotch chips, coconut, and pecans (in that order) over the sweetened condensed milk.
5 Bake at 350° for 25 to 30 minutes, or until it looks done (the coconut turns a nice brown).
6 Remove from the oven and *let cool*. If you cut it too soon, it's entirely too gooey. Once it's well cooled, it firms up and you can divide and conquer.

Snow-Covered Gingersnaps

Prep/cook time: 40 minutes   Makes 3–4 dozen

If I could only bake one kind of cookie, this recipe, which has been in our family since my mother was a child, would be my choice. It's delicious and keeps (and ships) well. The number of minutes you bake these cookies determines whether the cookies are soft or crispy. I prefer mine soft, so I bake them for 8 minutes. If you want a crisp cookie, bake them longer. The yield depends on how large you roll the balls—the larger you roll them, the fewer the cookies. At a request from a friend, in recent years I've experimented with making an **extra gingery version**. Crystallized ginger chips didn't work (the chips dissolved). Eventually I came up with something acceptably gingery: Use 7 teaspoons ginger (instead of 1), 1/4 cup minced fresh ginger, 2 teaspoons each cinnamon and cloves, and add another 1/8 cup molasses.

1/2 cup unsalted butter, softened	1 1/2 teaspoons baking soda
1 cup packed brown sugar	1/4 teaspoon salt
1/4 cup molasses	1 teaspoon ground cinnamon
1 large egg	1 teaspoon ground cloves
2 cups all-purpose flour	1 teaspoon ground ginger
	1 1/2 cups powdered sugar

1   Preheat oven to 350°.
2   Cream butter and brown sugar together.
3   Add molasses.
4   Mix in egg, flour, baking soda, salt, and spices in that order. The batter should be fine-grained and silky, not crumbly, holding together in a single ball. If it isn't, you may need to knead it a bit by hand.
5   Form into 1-inch balls and roll in powdered sugar.
6   Place balls on a baking sheet lined with a silicone mat (or just use an ungreased baking sheet). **Do not flatten the cookies**. If you are preparing the cookies in a warm room (above 66°), put the baking sheet in the refrigerator for 20 minutes.
7   Bake for 8 minutes (up to 12 minutes if you want a crisper cookie), or until cookies start to crackle on top and spring back slightly when touched with your fingertip.
8   Remove from oven and cool on wire racks.

Custards, Mousses, and Ice Cream

When you put cream and eggs together, you get delicious desserts: custards, ice creams, mousses, puddings, souffles, and so on. I've included several never-fail favorites of that sort in this chapter, plus a few recipes that don't quite fit in any other chapter in this book. Try my own Green Tea Ice Cream (page 95), which, if I do say so myself, is better than anything store-bought, and the Peppermint Ice Cream (page 97).

About Scalding Milk

Some recipes in this book, and especially in this chapter, call for you to scald the milk. To scald milk, bring the milk to just under a boil (180°). In the days before pasteurized milk, scalding milk destroyed bacteria and an enzyme that prevents thickening. You don't normally need to scald milk nowadays, though it helps make custards smoother and, some say, makes better cakes and breads.

About Ice Cream

To make ice cream, you can use a hand-cranked ice cream machine, a pan in your freezer, or an electric machine, sometimes with a built-in compressor. However you make it, ice cream falls into two categories:

- Philadelphia style ice cream (also called American or New York style), made from cream (or sometimes milk, half-and-half, or a combination), sugar, and flavorings. Sometime it's also made with raw eggs.
- French style ice cream, made from eggs, cream and sugar cooked into a custard, then flavored.

Philadelphia style is fast and super easy. Many of my recipes are Philadelphia style with eggs added. If raw eggs are a concern, you can use pasteurized eggs. Philadelphia style ice cream tends to stay softer when frozen.

French style ice cream takes longer to make and requires a higher degree of skill and familiarity with making a custard to get it right. Custard-based ice creams also get quite firm upon freezing.

When making ice cream, don't skimp on the cream. You can substitute half and half or even milk, but the flavors and mouth feel won't be quite the same.

Speaking of mouth feel, sometimes your ice cream might leave a fatty coating in your mouth. If that happens, the likelihood is that you over churned the ice cream and some of the cream turned into butter. It's tempting to keep churning until the ice cream is hard, but resist. Try any of these solutions:

- Churn the ice cream only until it's of soft-serve consistency, then put it in your freezer to harden the rest of the way.
- Substitute milk or half-and-half for some of the cream.
- Add a tablespoon of instant milk powder, buttermilk powder, or lecithin, or add a raw egg.

If after trying some of this chapter's ice cream recipes, you want to explore further, two of the best ice cream books I've ever used are *Ben & Jerry's Homemade Ice Cream & Dessert Book*, by Ben Cohen, Jerry Greenfield, and Nancy Stevens (Turtleback, 1987); and Bruce Weinstein's *The Ultimate Ice Cream Book* (William Morrow and Company, 1999).

Making Ice Cream in the Freezer

In this book's introduction, I spoke briefly about ice cream machines. They make it so easy to make your own ice cream, and if you can afford one, I recommend getting one.

However, if you don't have an ice cream machine, you can use the freezer method for any of the ice cream recipes in this chapter.

To make ice cream in your freezer,

1   Make the ice cream as described in the recipe. When it says to freeze according to manufacturer's directions, instead cool the ice cream base in the refrigerator for about 30 minutes.
2   Once the mixture is cool, put it in a glass or metal dish with some room at the top for expansion and for stirring (a 9" loaf pan is often the right size). Cover tightly and put in the freezer.
3   Every 30 minutes, open the container and stir. (You're stirring to help prevent ice crystals from forming.) Keep doing this until the ice cream is frozen, about 3 to 4 hours.

Chai Spiced Ice Cream

Prep/cook time: 2 hours   Makes 1 quart

To create this ice cream, I modified the spice mixture from my own masala chai recipe and adapted the recipe for Ginger Maple Ice Cream (page 92). You can buy the spices, including the smoked black peppercorns, from Mountain Rose Herbs (MountainRoseHerbs.com). If you don't have smoked peppercorns, you can substitute regular black peppercorns. For all my recipes that call for whole spices, but for this one especially, don't use ground spices (with the exception of the nutmeg, which is really hard to grind yourself unless you have a heavy duty spice grinder). You just won't get the same lovely, complex, deeply layered flavors from pre-ground spices.

- 1 three-inch stick true cinnamon
- 1 teaspoon green cardamom (*Elettaria cardamomum*), decorticated
- 2 smoked black peppercorns
- 3 mace blades
- 4 whole allspice berries
- 1/4 teaspoon ground nutmeg

- 1 one-inch length fresh ginger, sliced thinly (no need to peel)
- 2 cups heavy cream, divided
- 1 cup whole milk
- 1/2 cup pure maple syrup
- 1/2 cup granulated sugar
- 1 teaspoon vanilla extract
- 1/8 teaspoon salt

1. Coarsely pound the whole spices in a mortar.
2. Put ginger slices in a non-reactive saucepan and barely cover with water.
3. Bring to a soft boil and simmer gently for one minute.
4. Drain, then add the spices to the ginger in the saucepan.
5. Combine 1 cup of the cream with the maple syrup and sugar. Stir well.
6. Add the cream mixture to the spices and warm gently for one minute.
7. Set aside to let cool for one hour.
8. Strain the cream mixture and discard the spices.
9. Mix the remaining cream, milk, vanilla, and salt, then add to the spiced cream. Stir well.
10. Process in your ice cream maker according to the manufacturer's directions.

Chocolate Mocha Mousse

Prep/cook time: 8 hours 45 minutes   Makes 4 servings

C hocolate and coffee taste wonderful together, though for my tastes, I prefer that the coffee not overwhelm the chocolate. If you don't have extra-large eggs, use 5 large eggs.

2 ounces semisweet chocolate	1¼ teaspoons unflavored
¼ cup water	gelatin
4 extra large eggs, separated	¼ cup coffee liqueur
½ cup granulated sugar	1 cup heavy cream
¼ cup cold water	2 tablespoons granulated sugar

1   Carefully melt chocolate and ¼ cup water in a small saucepan.
2   Whisk sugar into egg yolks until well mixed and pale yellow. Put egg yolk/sugar mix in the top of a double boiler, but don't start heating yet.
3   Add melted chocolate to egg yolks, then heat, stirring constantly, until mixture thickens to the consistency of a thin custard (about five minutes). Remove from heat.
4   Sprinkle gelatin over the cold water and let sit for 3 minutes.
5   Heat gelatin/water mix over medium heat until completely dissolved. Add to chocolate mixture.
6   Stir in coffee liqueur.
7   Chill mixture in refrigerator for 30 minutes.
8   Whip cream and fold into the chilled mixture.
9   Beat egg whites until they stand in stiff peaks and gently fold into mixture.
10 Pour into individual dessert glasses or into a baked pie shell or a serving dish. Chill for 8 hours or until set.

Ginger Maple Ice Cream

Prep/cook time: about 2 hours   Makes 1 quart

I modified this Philadelphia-style recipe (found on MmmIsForMommy.com) for simplicity and ease, then developed my own Chai Spiced Ice Cream (page 90) using the same modified methods.

1 three-inch length of fresh ginger, sliced thinly (no need to peel)
2 cups heavy cream, divided
½ cup pure maple syrup

½ cup granulated sugar
¼ teaspoon salt
1 cup whole milk
1 teaspoon vanilla extract

1   Place the sliced ginger in a non-reactive saucepan and barely cover with water.
2   Bring to a soft boil and simmer gently for one minute.
3   Drain ginger, discard the water, and put the ginger back into the same pan.
4   Add 1 cup of the heavy cream and all the maple syrup, sugar, and salt. Gently warm the mixture until the sugar dissolves. Don't let it boil.
5   Remove from heat and let sit for one hour, so the cream absorbs the ginger flavor.
6   In a separate bowl, combine the remaining cream, milk, and vanilla.
7   Strain the ginger-cream mixture into the cream, milk, and vanilla mixture and stir gently.
8   Process according to the directions for your ice cream maker.

Greek Orange Custard

Prep/cook time: 1 hour 30 minutes   Makes one 13" x 9" panful

This deliciously different recipe is an orange-flavored version of a Greek egg custard called *galatopeta*. When you make *galatopeta* with phyllo, it's called *galatoboureko*; I've included directions for making that, too. The original recipe, which I've changed a lot, is in Eva Zane's incomparable *Greek Cooking for the Gods*. Serve warm or chilled.

Ingredients for the Custard

4 cups whole milk
¼ cup unsalted butter (plus another ½ cup if you are making the phyllo version)
⅓ cup granulated sugar
½ cup uncooked farina
4 large eggs, beaten

12 sheets of phyllo (only for the phyllo version)
3 tablespoons orange juice concentrate, undiluted
1 teaspoon vanilla extract
1 teaspoon ground cinnamon

Ingredients for the Syrup

2 cups water
1 cup honey
1 cup granulated sugar
1 stick cinnamon

8 whole cloves
juice of 1 lemon
zest of 1 orange

Making the Custard

1   Preheat oven to 400°. Butter a 13" x 9" baking pan.
2   Scald the milk in a large saucepan (180°). Stir in butter and sugar. Gradually add the farina, stirring constantly. Slowly bring mixture to a boil.
3   When the mixture boils, remove from heat.
4   Slowly stir hot farina mixture into the eggs. Add orange juice concentrate and vanilla.
5   If you wish to use phyllo, skip now to the instructions under Making Greek Orange Custard with Phyllo (page 94) and finish making this dessert from there. Otherwise, continue with these instructions.
6   Pour custard into prepared pan and bake for 10 minutes at 400°.
7   Reduce heat to 350° and bake for another 45 minutes. While the custard is baking, make the syrup.

Making the Syrup

1   Place all syrup ingredients except the lemon juice and orange zest into a large saucepan. Bring to a boil, then lower heat and simmer 10 minutes.
2   Remove from heat and set aside to cool.
3   When it is cool, stir in lemon juice and orange zest.

Finishing the Custard

1   When custard comes out of the oven, cool the custard for 10 minutes.
2   Cut the custard into squares, then pour cooled syrup over the top and sprinkle with cinnamon.

Making Greek Orange Custard with Phyllo

1   Make the custard as describe under Greek Orange Custard (page 93) up to step 5.
2   Individually butter five sheets of phyllo with unsalted butter. Put the sheets in the 13" x 9" pan, then add a sixth sheet (don't butter this one).
3   Pour in the custard, then fold the edges of the phyllo over the custard.
4   Top the custard with five more individually buttered phyllo sheets and one unbuttered sheet (you'll butter that one in a bit).
5   Using the bottom layers of phyllo, gently pull the custard away from the edges of the pan. Tuck the top layers of phyllo between the sides of the bottom layers and the sides of the pan.
6   Butter the top layer. Score the top sheets into squares, diamonds, or triangles before baking.
7   Bake for 10 minutes at 400°. Reduce heat to 350° and bake for another 45 minutes.
8   While the custard is baking, make the syrup (as described above).
9   Immediately upon removing the custard from the oven, cut through the score marks down to the bottom of the pan.
10 Cool the custard on a rack for 10 minutes, then pour the cooled orange syrup over the top and sprinkle with cinnamon.

Green Tea Ice Cream

Prep/cook time: 1 hour   Makes about 1 quart

I love green tea ice cream, but have never found a commercial one that tastes good, so I developed my own recipe. The main ingredient is matcha, a powdered green tea that's central to the Japanese tea ceremony. Matcha is expensive because of how it is made. The tea plant is shaded before the harvest to increase the production of the amino acids that make the tea taste sweeter. Harvested by hand, the leaves are dried and powdered to produce matcha.

1½ cups granulated sugar
¼ cup powdered green tea
    (matcha)

4 large eggs
1½ cups half-and-half
1½ cups heavy cream

1   Combine the sugar and the matcha. Set aside.
2   In a large bowl, beat the eggs by hand until they are fairly light.
3   Gradually stir the sugar/tea mixture into the eggs until evenly mixed.
4   Add the half-and-half and cream, stirring until well mixed.
5   Chill, then freeze according to the directions for your ice cream maker (about 30 minutes). You may need to divide the mix into two equal amounts to freeze.

Meyer Lemon Ice Cream

Prep/cook time: 1 hour   Makes 1 quart

A smooth and creamy ice cream inspired by my Meyer lemon tree's gorgeous lemons and Bruce Weinstein's Lemon Ice Cream recipe in *The Ultimate Ice Cream Book*. The results taste like lemon meringue pie. If you use eggs from local, pastured chickens, whose eggs have gorgeous deep yellow yolks, the ice cream will be spectacularly lovely. You can use regular lemons if you don't have Meyer lemons.

2 large eggs, lightly beaten   **2** tablespoons unsalted butter
1 cup granulated sugar   **2** cups heavy cream
½ cup Meyer lemon juice   zest of two Meyer lemons

1   Combine the eggs, sugar, lemon juice, and butter in a double boiler. Bring water in the bottom part of the double boiler to a boil.
2   Stir constantly over heat for about 15 minutes or until the mixture thickens (it will coat a spoon).
3   Remove from heat and cool about five minutes.
4   Quickly and thoroughly stir the cream into the custard mix.
5   Cool in refrigerator for two hours.
6   Process according to the ice cream machine manufacturer's instructions. When the ice cream is a few minutes from being done, carefully sprinkle the lemon zest over the ice cream, then finish processing.

Peppermint Ice Cream

Prep/cook time: 1 hour   Makes about 2½ quarts

Peppermint is my favorite ice cream flavor, but it's hard to find outside the month of December. This French style recipe (adapted from Bruce Weinstein's *The Ultimate Ice Cream Book*) makes a delicious and refreshing peppermint ice cream that you can enjoy year-round.

1 cup heavy cream	1 tablespoon cornstarch
2 teaspoons peppermint extract	2 cups half-and-half
¾ cup granulated sugar	Burgundy food coloring (optional)
2 large eggs, beaten	23 round peppermint candies

1   Combine the peppermint extract and the cream in a small bowl; set aside.
2   Beat the sugar and eggs in a medium bowl until the mixture is thickened and pale yellow. Stir in the cornstarch and set aside.
3   Put the half-and-half in a double boiler and bring to a bare simmer. When the half-and-half is hot, remove it from heat and slowly mix ¼ cup into the sugar/egg mixture. Then gradually stir the remainder of the half-and-half into the sugar/egg mix.
4   Pour the sugar/egg/half-and-half mixture back into the double boiler and heat, stirring constantly, until the custard thickens slightly. Don't let it boil.
5   Remove the double boiler from the stove and strain the mixture into a clean bowl. (If you used a stand mixer to mix the sugar and eggs together, pour the mixture back into the same bowl.)
6   Let the custard sit 15 minutes, then stir in the cream/peppermint mixture.
7   Slowly stir in the desired amount of food coloring. A little goes a long way, so be careful! Add just a tiny bit at first and stir well after each addition, adding only a drop or two at a time until it reaches the desired pink color.
8   Cool the custard completely, then process in your ice cream machine according to the manufacturer's instructions.
9   While the custard is processing, unwrap the peppermint candies and crack them into small pieces. The best way to crack them is to pulse-whir them in a strong blender, such as a VitaMix, on

the low setting. Smallish cracked pieces are the best; you don't want it crushed to a powder or the candy will dissolve in the ice cream. To crack the candies by hand, wrap the unwrapped candies in a sturdy, clean cloth towel and crack with a hammer or wooden rolling pin.

10 When the ice cream is five minutes away from being done, add the candy. If you are freezing the entire batch of custard at once, add all the candy. If you are freezing it in two equal batches, add half the candy per batch.

11 When the ice cream is done, serve immediately (it will be soft), or place in a container and freeze.

Rice Pudding

Prep/cook time: 1 hour 20 minutes   Makes one 13" x 9" pan

U se any kind of cooked rice (brown, white, red, or black; basmati, and so on), and any combination of milk, cream, or half-and-half; experiment to find what you prefer. This recipe is very forgiving of variations in amounts and can be made with just about any quantity of rice, so if you don't have 5 cups of leftover rice, try the following proportions: For each cup of cooked rice, use 2 eggs, 1 cup milk, ¼ cup cream, ½ teaspoon vanilla, ¼ teaspoon cinnamon, ⅛ teaspoon nutmeg, and 3 tablespoons honey. As you increase the amount of rice, decrease the number of eggs. Be sure to use the right-sized baking pan. Serve warm or cold with cream or whipped cream on top—heavenly!

8 large eggs, beaten well
3 cups whole milk or half-and-half
1 cup heavy cream
2 teaspoons vanilla extract

1½ teaspoons ground cinnamon
½ teaspoon ground nutmeg
¾ cup honey
5 cups cooked rice
1 cup raisins (optional)

1   Place eggs in a large bowl. Add the milk, cream, vanilla, cinnamon, nutmeg, and honey. Blend well.
2   Stir in the rice and raisins.
3   Place in a well-buttered 13" x 9" pan. Optionally, you can place the pan of rice pudding into a bain-marie (a slight larger pan filled with hot water).
4   Bake at 325° for an hour, or until the pudding is nicely browned and a knife inserted near the middle comes out cleanly.

Rich Chocolate Pudding

Prep/cook time: 30 minutes   Makes 12 small servings

Serve this exceedingly dense and rich pudding in very small individual ramekins—even the most ardent chocolate lovers will appreciate a smaller serving. You can substitute other flavors of chips (butterscotch chips, white chocolate
chips, mint chocolate chips, and so on) for the chocolate chips. For a cocoa-based
pudding, see the recipe for Chocolate Cream Pie (page 128). This recipe tells how
to make this pudding using a microwave (one of my very few exceptions to using
a microwave); you can also cook it in a heavy saucepan or a double boiler on the
stovetop. Serve warm or cool with heavy or whipped cream.

1 cup granulated sugar	**1** ounce unsweetened baking
3 tablespoons cornstarch	chocolate, melted
3 cups whole milk	**3** tablespoons unsalted butter
3 large egg yolks, lightly beaten	**1½** teaspoons vanilla extract
1½ cups chocolate chips	

1   Combine sugar and cornstarch in a 3-quart bowl, mixing
    thoroughly. Whisk in milk.
2   Microwave at full power, whisking every 4 minutes, for 10 to 12
    minutes or until mixture is thickened and bubbly.
3   Remove from microwave and add chocolate chips and baking
    chocolate.
4   Return to microwave and microwave at full power for 1 minute.
5   Remove from microwave and stir until the chocolate is melted.
    Stir a small amount of the hot mixture into the beaten egg yolks,
    then stir the egg yolk mixture into the hot mixture.
6   Return to microwave and microwave at full power for 1 minute
    more or until thickened.
7   Remove from microwave and whisk.
8   Stir in butter until melted.
9   Stir in vanilla.
10 Pour into small ramekins and chill.

Spiced Bavarian Cream

Prep/cook time: 3 hours   Makes 6 servings

Bavarian cream, also known as *crème Bavarois* or just *Bavarois*, is a firmer relative of Boston cream (such as in the Boston Cream Pie on page 17). Bavarian cream is often used as a filling; here, it's a very rich dessert that stands on its own.

3½ cups whole milk
4½ to 5 teaspoons (2 envelopes) unflavored gelatin
6 large eggs, separated
¾ cup granulated sugar
⅛ teaspoon salt
½ teaspoon ground ginger

¼ teaspoon ground nutmeg
¼ teaspoon ground cardamom
1½ teaspoons vanilla extract
1 cup heavy cream
1 cup fresh berries or fruit (for garnish)

1   Scald 3 cups of milk (180°) and set aside.
2   Mix gelatin into the remaining ½ cup of milk and set aside.
3   Beat egg yolks, sugar, salt, and spices. Slowly add scalded milk to egg yolk mixture.
4   Place mixture in a heavy-bottomed saucepan or the top half of a double boiler. Heat, stirring constantly, until the custard thickens.
5   Add the softened gelatin to the custard, stirring until the gelatin dissolves.
6   Add vanilla.
7   Remove from heat and chill the custard until slightly thickened.
8   While the custard is cooling, beat egg whites until they stand in stiff peaks.
9   Whip the cream. Set aside 4 tablespoons of the whipped cream.
10 Fold egg whites and remaining whipped cream into the custard.
11 Spoon into a 2½ quart mold or bowl. Chill until firm.
12 Remove from mold and garnish with the reserved whipped cream and the fruit and berries.

Steamed Bread Pudding

Prep/cook time: 1 hour 35 minutes   Makes 10 servings

I'll be forever grateful to Frances Buran, whom I first met while working at Borland in the late 1980s, for this recipe: a delicious dessert plus a way to use up leftover bread! I've greatly simplified her original recipe. I often use whole grain breads, which make for a rich and tasty dessert, though plain croissants are marvelous. Try your own variations with the bread (or other ingredients). Walnuts, pecan, and almonds are wonderful in this pudding. Serve warm topped with heavy cream or whipped cream.

4 large eggs, lightly beaten
2 cups whole milk or half-and-half
1 tablespoon ground cinnamon
½ cup packed brown sugar
1½ cups chocolate chips
4 cups bread cubes
½ cup chopped nuts

1 In a large mixing bowl, combine the eggs, milk, cinnamon, brown sugar, chocolate chips, and nuts.
2 Stir in the dry bread cubes and make sure all the cubes are soaked.
3 Pour into an ungreased 9" x 7" x 2½" baking dish. Push down any cubes of bread that are poking up too high out of the mixture.
4 Place the filled baking dish into a 13" x 9" x 2" pan set on the oven rack. Pour hot water into the larger pan to the depth of one inch, being careful not to spill any water into the bread pudding.
5 Bake, uncovered, at 350° for 60 to 65 minutes or until a knife inserted near the center of the pudding comes out clean.

Frostings and Sweet Sauces

T he category of sauces covers a wide range of liquids, from savory to sweet, that are used to enhance food. In addition to frostings and icing (the main subject of this chapter), sweet sauces include such things as butterscotch sauce, chocolate sauce, fruit sauces (made with strawberries or other types of berries), Crème Anglais, and so on. Savory sauces include such things as gravies, salsa, and pesto.

In this chapter, I've included my favorite, never-fail frostings and sweet sauces. Frostings are usually (though not always) made with sugar, butter, and flavorings, and are spread on cakes, cake-like desserts, and cookies. The word icing is sometimes used interchangeably with frosting, though sometimes "icing" is taken to mean a thinner, more liquid form of frosting.

Frostings come in several varieties, each with its own many variations: buttercreams (a soft frosting), fondant (a firmer, clay-like frosting that you can roll out—a favorite for wedding cakes; in the UK, this kind of frosting is called sugar paste), ganache (a rich chocolate icing made with cream and chocolate and not much else), and royal icing (a hard, usually white icing).

A frosting should complement the cake in both appearance and flavor. Lighter frostings are pleasing when contrasted with a darker cake and vice versa. For example, basic buttercream looks lovely on a dark chocolate cake. A rich dark chocolate frosting is tantalizing on a yellow cake. For complementary flavors, use sweeter frostings on less-sweet cakes; use tangy or less-sweet frostings on sweeter cakes or on fruit- or vegetable-based cakes.

Some cakes are great with just a dusting of powdered sugar. For a nice touch, sift the powdered sugar through a lace doily placed on a dark cake or on gingerbread (then remove the doily).

In addition to the frostings and glazes in this chapter, other desserts have their own sweet sauce, frosting, icing, or syrup recipes—check the index under "frostings and sweet sauces."

About Buttercream Frostings

Most of the recipes in this chapter are variations on the basic buttercream frosting. In the baking community, you'll find the phrase "buttercream frosting" used for a variety of ingredients and techniques, falling into the six categories shown in the following table.

Six types of buttercream frostings

Type of buttercream	Other names	Made with
basic	American	butter, sugar, cream
flour	boiled milk or ermine icing	sweet flour pudding base and butter
French	—	egg yolk foam and hot sugar syrup
German	—	sweet custard base and butter
Italian	—	meringue made with egg whites, sugar, and water
Swiss	Swiss meringue buttercream	meringue made with egg whites and sugar

Basic Buttercream Frosting

Prep/cook time: 15 minutes   Makes enough to frost a 13" x 9" cake

You can use this easy buttercream recipe as a base for your own variations. For example, add cocoa, replace the vanilla with brandy, or add some ground cardamom. Cardamom is fantastic in this recipe, but be careful! Cardamom gets stronger as it sits, so use much less than you think you need.

1 cup unsalted butter, softened
1 teaspoon vanilla extract
4 cups powdered sugar

2 to 4 tablespoons heavy cream, half-and-half, or whole milk

1   In a large bowl, cream butter until light.
2   Mix in the vanilla and one tablespoon of the cream.
3   Gradually add powdered sugar, beating well after each addition, tasting as you go. You don't want the flavor to be sweet and nothing else.
4   When the frosting starts to get dry, add the remaining cream and beat until light.

Bittersweet Chocolate Frosting

Prep/cook time: 30 minutes   Makes about 1½ cups

Fabulous frosting. Essentially a simplified German buttercream made without milk, this recipe uses granulated sugar rather than powdered. Like many chocolate recipes, this one benefits from a tiny amount of salt.

1 cup granulated sugar	**1** tablespoon unsalted butter
3 tablespoons cornstarch	**1** teaspoon vanilla extract
⅛ teaspoon salt	**3** ounces unsweetened
1 cup water	chocolate

1   Combine sugar, cornstarch, and salt in a saucepan. Mix well.
2   Add water and stir.
3   Place over medium heat and cook, stirring constantly, until thickened and clear (about 10 minutes).
4   Remove from heat; add butter, vanilla, and chocolate. Stir until chocolate is melted. Cool in refrigerator before using.

Caramel Sauce

Prep/cook time: 30 minutes   Makes about 1½ cups

When my daughter discovered how easy it is to make caramel sauce, we were liberated from buying the store-bought stuff. You can use this recipe in the Caramel Crunch Bars (page 70) or as a topping for ice cream, brownies, fresh apple slices, or any other thing you would drizzle caramel sauce on. Because this sauce is mostly sugar, it should last in the refrigerator up to two weeks, but always practice good food hygiene and safety, and discard if you suspect it's spoiled. The cream of tartar helps prevent crystallization.

1 cup granulated sugar   ½ cup heavy cream
3 tablespoons water   **4** tablespoons butter, cut up
⅛ teaspoon cream of tartar   ½ teaspoon kosher salt

1   Important! Have all ingredients ready before you start. Things move slowly at first, then very quickly.
2   Combine sugar, water, and cream of tartar in a medium saucepan. Stir to dissolve sugar.
3   Bring to a boil over medium-high heat.
4   Once it starts reaches a straw color, turn the heat to low, but keep it simmering.
5   Cook to between 360° and 375° degrees.
6   When it reaches a lovely brown caramel color, quickly stir in the butter and cream. It'll fizz up.
7   Stir in the salt, then remove from heat. The caramel should be smooth and glossy. Use immediately or refrigerate until needed.

Chocolate Fudge Sauce

Prep/cook time: 10 minutes   Makes ¾ cup

You can use this versatile recipe, my own invention, as a topping for ice cream. Cooled, it makes a dense, rich pudding. Adjust quantities of cream and water to make it thicker or thinner, and quantities of sugar to make it more or less sweet. If you thin it with a lot of milk, it makes an incredibly rich hot cocoa drink.

3 tablespoons cocoa powder
9 tablespoons granulated sugar
2 tablespoons water
¼ cup heavy cream

2 teaspoons unsalted butter
dash cayenne pepper
1 teaspoon vanilla extract

1   Combine the cocoa and sugar in a small saucepan.
2   Add water. Stir until everything is uniform.
3   Add cream, butter, and cayenne. Heat over medium heat, stirring constantly, until the sauce is smooth. Don't let it boil.
4   Stir in vanilla. Use immediately or cool and use later.

Chocolate Glaze

Prep/cook time: 15 minutes

Makes enough glaze for one 10" Bundt cake

T his simple and easy recipe is great as a glaze for a Bundt cake. It's smooth, thin, and shiny.

2 cups powdered sugar
1 tablespoon unsalted butter, softened

2 tablespoons cocoa powder
½ teaspoon vanilla extract
2 to 4 tablespoons whole milk

1   Combine sugar, butter, and cocoa.
2   Add vanilla.
3   Add milk gradually to achieve a smooth, thickened consistency.
4   Stir until smooth.

Chocolate Sour Cream Frosting

Prep/cook time: 15 minutes   Makes about 1½ cups

 A tangy, less sweet frosting; suitable for spicy cakes or cupcakes. Try it on Honey Spice Cupcakes (page 33).

12 ounces semisweet   **1** cup sour cream
chocolate, melted

1   Combine chocolate and sour cream and mix well.

Chocolate Whipped Cream Filling

Prep/cook time: 1 hour

Makes enough filling for one 9" layer cake

Use this simple recipe as a filling layer in a cake, or to fill eclairs or cream puffs as well. These are essentially the same ingredients as a ganache, only with more cream than chocolate (a ganache has more chocolate than cream) and with the melted chocolate folded into the whipped cream rather than the chocolate being melted in the cream.

1 cup heavy cream

8 ounces German's sweet chocolate, melted and cooled to room temperature

1   Whip cream.
2   Fold melted, cooled chocolate into whipped cream.
3   Chill 15 to 20 minutes before using.

Cream Cheese Frosting

Prep/cook time: 10 minutes   Makes 4 cups

Cream cheese frosting is a classic for such cakes as carrot and red velvet. Try this frosting on Food of the Gods Carrot Cake on page 27, Gingerbread (page 29), or Cocoa Apple Cake (page 24). The difference between a good cream cheese frosting and a great one is in the whipping. In the words of the immortal Devo, "Whip it good."

½ cup unsalted butter, softened
8 ounces cream cheese, room
temperature

2 teaspoons vanilla extract
⅛ teaspoon salt
3 cups powdered sugar

1   Beat butter and cream cheese until very well blended and creamy.
2   Add the vanilla and salt and blend in a minute more.
3   Carefully add the powdered sugar one cup at a time and beat very, very well, until the frosting is light. It will go through a dense stage—keep beating. Once it's light and fluffy, it's done.

Fluffy Chocolate Buttercream Frosting

Prep/cook time: 15 minutes   Makes about 2 cups

One of my favorite frostings. Like the Tender Fudge Layer Cake (page 38), this recipe came from the March 1976 *Woman's Day* magazine (as the frosting for that cake). It doesn't make enough to frost a two-layer 9" cake, though; you'll need to double the recipe. Beating the frosting over a bowl of ice and water is the secret to the fluffiness.

½ cup unsalted butter,
    softened
3 ounces unsweetened
    chocolate, melted

2½ cups powdered sugar
4 tablespoons hot water
1 teaspoon vanilla extract

1   Cream butter.
2   Add the melted chocolate.
3   Gradually beat in sugar alternately with hot water.
4   Add vanilla.
5   Place bowl inside a larger bowl of ice and water and beat until fluffy.

Fudgy Buttercream Frosting

Prep/cook time: 10 minutes   Makes 2 cups

This makes a dense, fudgy frosting. Try it on a yellow cake for visual contrast.

½ cup butter, softened
1½ cups powdered sugar
⅛ teaspoon salt

3 ounces unsweetened
    chocolate, melted
2 teaspoons vanilla extract

1   Cream butter and powdered sugar until light and fluffy.
2   Add salt and melted chocolate.
3   Add vanilla. Continue beating until shiny and smooth.

Hard Sauce

Prep/cook time: 10 minutes   Makes 2 cups

More like a thick frosting than a sauce. A classic topping for fruitcake and other holiday desserts. Korbel, a champagne cellar in Sonoma County, California, makes an excellent brandy that's delicious in this recipe.

½ cup unsalted butter,
   softened
3 cups powdered sugar

⅛ teaspoon salt
⅓ cup brandy, whiskey, or rum

1 Cream the butter.
2 Gradually add sugar, mixing well.
3 Add salt and brandy and continue to beat until firm and fluffy. Taste to make sure it's the appropriate and desired proof.

Hot Gingerbread Icing

Prep/cook time: 10 minutes   Makes ½ cup

This is my mother's recipe. She would spread it on top of her delicious Gingerbread (page 29) while the cake was still warm from the oven.

2 tablespoons unsalted butter   **2** tablespoons condensed milk
1 teaspoon ground ginger   powdered sugar

1   Mix butter, ginger, and milk together.
2   Beat in enough powdered sugar to make a smooth liquid icing.

Mocha Buttercream Frosting

Prep/cook time: 20 minutes   Makes 5 cups

Yum! A frosting for mocha lovers. Makes enough to frost a three-layer 9" cake.

½ cup unsalted butter,
    softened
5 cups powdered sugar

¼ cup cocoa powder
2 teaspoons vanilla extract
¼ cup hot, strong coffee

1   Beat butter until smooth.
2   Combine the powdered sugar and cocoa.
3   Gradually add powdered sugar/cocoa mix to the butter, mixing
    constantly. Mixture will be dry.
4   Add vanilla and coffee. Beat until smooth.

Orange Icing

Prep/cook time: 15 minutes   Makes 2½ cups

A super simple frosting and an interesting taste sensation on Gingerbread (page 29). Also perfect with Orange Layer Cake (page 36).

¼ cup unsalted butter,
    softened
3½ cups powdered sugar

juice of one orange (pulp and
    all)
whole milk as needed

1   Cream butter and sugar together, then beat in orange juice.
2   Continue mixing until of a smooth consistency. Add a little milk if
    necessary.

Ultimate Chocolate Frosting

Prep/cook time: 10 minutes   Makes 2¾ cups

It's a bit of hyperbole to call this recipe "ultimate." Other recipes, such as the Fluffy Chocolate Buttercream Frosting (page 113), are equally excellent. However, that's the original name for this recipe, which I've had for decades and no longer remember the source, and it is indeed wonderful. Try it with Chocolate Cardamom Cake (page 20). If you like a thick layer of frosting, you might need to one-and-a-half or double this recipe to frost a 9" two-layer cake.

½ cup unsalted butter, softened
¾ cup cocoa powder
3½ cups powdered sugar

6 to 7 tablespoons heavy cream or whole milk
1 teaspoon vanilla extract

1   Cream butter.
2   Add cocoa carefully. (If you're using a mixer, if you're not careful, cocoa will fly everywhere.)
3   Alternately adding the sugar and cream, beat until of spreading consistency. Add more cream if needed.
4   Add vanilla. Beat until silky.

Pies and Tarts

You can find entire books devoted just to pies, proving that we humans have a deep love for all things pie related. Pies—filled dough crusts—come in many shapes and with a variety of fillings, both savory and sweet, and have been around for millennia. According to the American Pie Council (PieCouncil.org), the first pies in history came from the ancient Egyptians, who passed along the idea to the Greeks, who in turn shared the idea with the Romans.

The earliest written pie recipe we have, the American Pie Council informs us, is a rye-crusted goat cheese and honey pie published in ancient Rome. That sounds seriously delicious. Sam Worley, an intrepid writer at Epicurious.com, thought so too, and did his best to track down the recipe. The closest he came was a recipe in Cato's *De Agricultura 76*. Because the recipe is incomplete, Sam constructed his own version. I'm sure you're just as intrigued as I was when I first found this out; here's a link to his recipe: Epicurious.com/recipes/food/views/goat-cheese-honey-and-rye-crust-pie.

In this chapter, I've included only sweet pies (this being, after all, a dessert cookbook), along with a perfect no-lard, no-shortening pie crust recipe I spent a few years perfecting. I've also included my apple-berry crisp recipe, which isn't a pie, though you could use the filling in a pie or tarts.

Apple-Berry Crisp

Prep/cook time: 1 hour   Makes a three-quart crisp

A crisp (also sometimes called a crumble) is fruit topped with a flour-oatmeal mixture and baked. Butter, sugar, and spices are also involved. I threw this together one day, winging it without a recipe. I didn't use flour, so it's gluten free. Although I love true cinnamon (Ceylon cinnamon, *Cinnamomum verum*; using the Latin names ensures you get the right thing), cassia cinnamon (*Cinnamomum cassia*) works best in this recipe. Use any variety of apple that appeals to you. I never peel apples, but you can peel them if you like. Serve hot with ice cream (vanilla or ginger), or serve cold with heavy cream.

Ingredients for the Filling

5 cups apples, cored, sliced, and cut into 1-inch cubes
½ cup water
1 tablespoon unsalted butter
1 tablespoon brown sugar

½ teaspoon ground cinnamon
4 cups frozen berries (I use blueberries, blackberries, and raspberries, but any berries will do)

Ingredients for the Topping

3 cups rolled oats
⅓ cup packed brown sugar
4 teaspoons ground cinnamon
½ teaspoon ground nutmeg

½ teaspoon ground allspice
¼ teaspoon ground cloves
6 tablespoons unsalted butter, melted

1   Place the apples and water in a three-quart range-top-safe casserole dish.
2   Slice the tablespoon of butter and dot the slices on the apples.
3   Cook over medium heat, stirring occasionally, until the apples are softened, but still firm. Remove from heat.
4   Stir in the brown sugar and cinnamon, then stir in the berries.
5   Combine the dry topping ingredients and mix well.
6   Pour the melted butter over the oat mixture and stir well.
7   Carefully smooth the topping over the fruit mixture.
8   Place casserole dish on a baking sheet (to catch any spills).
9   Cover the casserole dish and bake at 350° for 35 to 45 minutes.

Berry Pie

Prep/cook time: 1 hour   Makes one 9" pie

Although this recipe calls for fresh berries, frozen berries work great too—just cook the pie a little longer and increase the flour to ⅓ cup. I used to make this with fructose, but decided I prefer sugar. Serve hot or cold with heavy cream or ice cream. Try my Perfect Pie Crust (page 136) for the crust.

Ingredients for the Pie

crust for one 9" pie (top and bottom)

1 quart ripe berries (one kind or a mixture), washed, hulled, drained, and dried

1 cup granulated sugar

¼ cup all-purpose flour or 2½ tablespoons cornstarch or arrowroot

⅛ teaspoon salt

1 teaspoon orange or lemon zest

2 tablespoons unsalted butter

Ingredients for the Glaze

1 tablespoon whole milk   2 teaspoons granulated sugar

1   Preheat oven to 425°.
2   Put bottom half of crust into a 9" pie pan; don't trim the edge.
3   Roll top crust, cut steam slits in the center, and cover with cloth while you prepare the filling. (Alternatively, if you want to make a fancier-looking pie, cut the top crust into strips and weave the strips into a lattice top when putting on the top crust.)
4   Place berries in a bowl and sprinkle with the 1 cup of sugar and all of the flour, salt, and citrus zest. Toss gently. Taste berries; if too tart, add more sugar.
5   Spoon berry mix into the bottom pie shell and dot with butter.
6   Brush pastry rim with cold water.
7   Fit top crust over berries, trim, seal, and crimp edges. For a glistening crust, brush milk on top crust of pie, then sprinkle with sugar.
8   Bake 35 to 45 minutes until lightly browned and bubbling.
9   Cool 5 to 10 minutes before cutting.

Chocolate Bourbon Hazelnut Pie

Prep/cook time: 1½ to 2 hours   Makes one 9" pie

The filling for this gluten-free recipe is my adaptation of the Portland, Oregon Pacific Pie Co.'s amazingly delicious Chocolate Bourbon Hazelnut Pie recipe. For the crust, I modified *Bon Appetit*'s hazelnut crust recipe. I use America's Test Kitchen's gluten-free flour blend, though any gluten-free flour blend should work. If the flour blend you're using contains xanthan gum, omit the xanthan gum from this recipe. This recipe takes fine timing but is otherwise fast, easy, and worth it. First, put the pie pan in the refrigerator. While the pan is chilling, make the hazelnut pie crust, then bake it in the chilled pan. Make the filling while the crust is baking. You want to pour the filling into the crust while the crust is still hot and the filling is still slightly warm. For a non-gluten-free crust, replace the gluten-free flour and xanthan gum with 1 cup all-purpose flour. You'll benefit from using a food processor for this recipe.

Ingredients for the Crust

¾ cup toasted, unsalted hazelnuts
1 cup gluten-free flour
¼ teaspoon xanthan gum
2 tablespoons granulated sugar

½ teaspoon Himalayan pink salt
½ cup unsalted butter, cold, cut into pieces
2 tablespoons sour cream
¾ teaspoon rice wine vinegar

Ingredients for the Filling

1 cup granulated sugar
⅔ cup brown rice syrup
⅓ cup maple syrup
½ cup unsalted butter
4 large eggs
¼ cup bourbon
1 teaspoon vanilla extract

¼ teaspoon Himalayan pink salt
1⅓ cup toasted, unsalted hazelnuts
¾ cup dark chocolate, chopped, or ¾ cup semisweet chocolate chips

Making the Pie Crust

1 Preheat oven to 350°. Put a 9" pie pan in the refrigerator to chill.
2 Pulse the gluten-free flour, xanthan gum, sugar, salt, and the ¾ cup toasted hazelnuts in a food processor until the consistency of coarse meal, about five minutes.

3   Add butter, sour cream, and vinegar to dry ingredients and mix until the dough holds together.
4   Remove chilled pie pan from refrigerator. Using your fingers, form the crust by pressing dough to the sides and bottom of the pan; make it smooth and evenly thick.
5   Chill the crust 20 minutes, then bake at 350° until golden but not completely baked (about 15 to 20 minutes).

Making the Filling

1   While the crust is baking, make the filling.
2   In a medium saucepan, combine sugar, brown rice syrup, maple syrup, and butter. Cook over medium heat until butter melts and sugar dissolves. Cool until barely warm.
3   In a large bowl, combine eggs, bourbon, vanilla, and salt. Whisk well to combine.
4   Slowly stir in the sugar mixture.
5   Cool until only slightly warm. The sugar/egg mixture should still be warmish, but not too warm. If the sugar/egg mixture is too hot, the chocolate will melt. You don't want that. You want distinct bits of soft chocolate.
6   Coarsely chop the 1⅓ cup hazelnuts, then stir the chopped nuts and chocolate into the sugar/egg mixture.
7   Pour the filling into the still-hot pie shell.
8   Bake 45 to 55 minutes until filling is set, though still slightly jiggly in the center. Cool completely before serving.

Chocolate Cheesecake

Prep/cook time: 1 hour 10 minutes plus   Makes one 10" pie
1 day

T his rich cheesecake gives 20 servings at least. To reduce the fat content, you
can use light cream cheese and light sour cream, and it'll be every bit as delicious. If kept covered and chilled, this cheesecake can keep for up to a week. Serve
with whipped cream.

Ingredients for the Crust

3 cups Famous Chocolate
  Wafers, crushed to a fine,
  even crumb

½ teaspoon ground cinnamon
¾ cup unsalted butter, melted

Ingredients for the Filling

1 cup granulated sugar
24 ounces cream cheese,
  softened
4 large eggs
1 pound semisweet chocolate,
  melted and slightly cooled
1 teaspoon vanilla extract

2 tablespoons cocoa powder
2 cups sour cream, room
  temperature
½ cup unsalted butter, melted
Semisweet chocolate bar for
  making curls

Making the Crust

1   Put crumbs into a medium bowl and mix thoroughly with
    cinnamon.
2   Blend in the butter.
3   Press crumbs firmly onto the bottom of a 10-inch springform
    pan.
4   Chill in the refrigerator while you make the filling.

Making the Filling

1   Preheat oven to 350°.
2   Beat sugar and cream cheese together in a large bowl until light
    and fluffy.
3   Add eggs one at a time, beating after each addition.
4   Add melted chocolate, vanilla, cocoa, and sour cream, beating
    constantly.
5   Add the butter and blend in thoroughly.

Putting It Together and Baking

1 Pour filling into the crust.
2 Bake on the lower rack of the oven for 45 to 50 minutes, or until the edges are completely set. The center may not appear set, but will firm as the cheesecake chills.
3 Remove from oven. Cool until warm on a wire rack, then cover and refrigerate overnight.
4 Just before serving, prepare the chocolate curls:

   • Hold a piece of semisweet chocolate in your hand until it is slightly warm.
   • Draw a vegetable parer over the surface of the chocolate to produce curls.

5 Remove the cheesecake from the pan and garnish with the chocolate curls.

Chocolate Cream Pie

Prep/cook time: 2½ hours   Makes one 9" pie

Almost every Thanksgiving, I make this family favorite as an alternative to pumpkin pie. If you want a perfect chocolate pudding, skip the crust, make the filling, and pour into individual ramekins (makes about six individual servings). For a denser pudding variation, see Rich Chocolate Pudding (page 100). This recipe is one of a few exceptions to my decision to not provide tool-specific instructions. Because the pudding part of this pie is so fast and foolproof to make in a microwave oven, I've included those instructions as well. Serve with whipped cream.

Ingredients for the Filling

11 graham crackers, crushed
½ cup unsalted butter, melted

1 tablespoon brown sugar

Ingredients for the Filling

1 cup granulated sugar
3 tablespoons cornstarch
⅛ teaspoon salt
¼ cup Dutch process cocoa powder
¼ cup natural cocoa powder

2 cups whole milk
1 cup heavy cream or half-and-half
3 large egg yolks, lightly beaten
1½ teaspoons vanilla extract

Making the Crust

1   Mix the graham cracker crumbs with the butter and brown sugar.
2   Pour the mix into a 9" pie pan.
3   Shape and flatten the crust, using a fork, the back of a spoon, or your hands.
4   Bake at 350° for 8 to 10 minutes.
5   Remove from oven and cool.

Stovetop Instructions for Making the Filling and Finishing the Pie

1   Combine sugar, cornstarch, salt, and cocoa powders in a medium saucepan. Mix thoroughly.
2   Whisk in milk and cream. Mix until no lumps of cocoa remain. (An immersion blender is excellent for removing the lumps.)
3   Cook on medium-high heat for about 20 minutes or until it thickens. Stir frequently to prevent burning and lumps.

4   Stir in a small amount of the hot mixture into the beaten egg yolks, then stir the egg yolk mixture into the hot mixture.
5   Cook three more minutes, stirring continuously, then remove from heat.
6   Stir in vanilla.
7   Pour into the pie crust and chill for 2 hours or until set.

Microwave Instructions for Making the Filling and Finishing the Pie

1   Make the crust as described earlier.
2   Combine sugar, cornstarch, salt, and cocoa in a 3-quart glass bowl. Mix thoroughly.
3   Whisk in milk and cream.
4   Microwave at full power, whisking at intervals. Whisk after 4 minutes, whisk after 4 more minutes, or 8 minutes total, and whisk after another 2 minutes, or 10 minutes total. It's ready for the next step when the mixture is thickened and bubbly.
5   Remove from microwave and whisk again.
6   Stir in a small amount of the hot mixture into the beaten egg yolks, then stir the egg yolk mixture into the hot mixture.
7   Microwave at full power for 1 minute more or until thickened. Remove from oven and whisk.
8   Stir in vanilla.
9   Pour into the pie crust and chill for 2 hours.

Chocolate Souffle Pie

Prep/cook time: 2½ hours   Makes one 9" pie

This fast, easy recipe is light, yet very satisfying—perfect for those times when you want something chocolate-y but you don't want something dense. You can also bake the filling in small individual tart pans. Serve with powdered sugar sprinkled over the top, or with whipped cream.

1 9-inch pie crust, unbaked	**1** tablespoon cocoa powder
2 cups heavy cream	**2** teaspoons granulated sugar
16 ounces semisweet chocolate	**2** large eggs, beaten
	2 teaspoons vanilla extract

1   Place the pie crust in a 9" pie pan. Set aside.
2   Scald the cream (180°). Remove from heat.
3   Carefully place the chocolate in the cream and let sit until the chocolate is melted enough to stir (a few minutes).
4   Stir the chocolate and cream until well mixed.
5   Add the cocoa, sugar, eggs, and vanilla extract one ingredient at a time, stirring well after each addition.
6   Pour mixture into the pie crust. Bake at 350° for 20 minutes or until the crust is golden.
7   Remove from heat and cool completely (about 1–2 hours).

Chocolate Walnut Pie

Prep/cook time: 2 hours   Makes one 9" pie

W alnuts and chocolate make this pie delectable without being too sweet. I wish I could recall which long-ago co-worker shared this recipe with me. Serve with whipped cream.

1 9-inch pie crust, unbaked	**⅛** teaspoon salt
2 to 3 tablespoons cold water	**1¼** cups honey
3 large eggs	**1** cup chocolate chips
½ cup granulated sugar	**⅔** cup coarsely chopped
1 teaspoon vanilla extract	walnuts

1   Preheat oven to 350° and put crust into a 9" pie pan.
2   In a large bowl, beat eggs.
3   Add sugar, vanilla, and salt; blend well.
4   Add honey; beat just until blended.
5   Stir in chocolate chips and walnuts.
6   Pour into pie crust.
7   Bake at 350° for 40 to 45 minutes or until filling is deep golden brown.
8   Cool at least 1 hour before serving.

Cranberry Pie

Prep/cook time: 1 hour   Makes one 9" pie

Serve warm with vanilla ice cream or whipped cream. You can also make this without the pie crust.

1 9-inch pie crust, unbaked
3 cups cranberries
3/4 cup chopped walnuts

1/2 cup plus 1/4 cup granulated
  sugar
1 large egg
1/2 cup all-purpose flour
1/3 cup unsalted butter, melted

1   Preheat oven to 325°.
2   Place the pie crust in a 9" pie pan.
3   Fill crust with cranberries.
4   Sprinkle cranberries with nuts and the 1/2 cup sugar.
5   Beat the egg with the remaining 1/4 cup sugar.
6   Add flour and butter to egg mixture and beat until no lumps remain.
7   Pour flour/egg mixture over cranberries.
8   Bake for 45 minutes, or until topping is a light golden brown.

Lemon Meringue Pie

Prep/cook time: 1 hour 15 minutes   Makes one 9" pie

I first made this pie in the late 1970s, trying out a healthier pie crust. The whole wheat crust is crumbly and rich, and the filling is delicious. You can use a regular pie crust if you want.

Ingredients for the Crust

1 scant cup whole wheat flour, or 1 scant cup all-purpose flour

$\frac{1}{2}$ teaspoon salt
$\frac{1}{3}$ cup unsalted butter
3 tablespoons cold water

Ingredients for the Lemon Filling

1$\frac{1}{2}$ cups granulated sugar
$\frac{1}{3}$ cup cornstarch
1$\frac{1}{2}$ cups water
3 large egg yolks, lightly beaten

3 tablespoons butter
zest of one lemon
$\frac{1}{4}$ cup lemon juice

Ingredient for the Meringue

3 large egg whites
$\frac{1}{4}$ teaspoon cream of tartar

6 tablespoons granulated sugar

Making the Crust

1   Mix flour and salt.
2   Cut in butter until well mixed.
3   Add cold water, a little at a time, until the dough is moist enough to stick together.
4   Form dough into a ball.
5   Flatten ball slightly with hands, then roll out to fit in a 9" pie pan. You may need to pat the dough in rather than roll it, because the whole wheat flour makes the dough a bit crumbly.
6   Put crust in a 9" pie pan.
7   Prick crust with fork and bake at 450° for 8 to 10 minutes.

Making the Filling

1   Mix sugar and cornstarch in a saucepan. Gradually stir in water.
2   Cook over medium heat, stirring constantly, until mixture thickens and boils.

3   Boil 1 minute, then remove from heat.
4   Slowly stir in half the hot mixture into the egg yolks, being
    careful not to cook the eggs.
5   Blend the egg yolks/hot mixture into the remaining hot mixture
    in the saucepan.
6   Return to the heat and boil 1 minute more, stirring constantly.
7   Remove from heat.
8   Add butter, lemon zest, and lemon juice.
9   Pour hot filling into baked pie crust.

Making the Meringue

1   Beat egg whites with cream of tartar until frothy.
2   Gradually beat in sugar, a little at a time.
3   Beat until the meringue is stiff and glossy and the sugar is
    dissolved.

Finishing the Pie

1   Pile the meringue onto the hot filling, carefully sealing the
    meringue onto the edge of the crust.
2   Bake at 400° for 8 to 10 minutes.

New York Style Cheesecake

Prep/cook time: 1½ hours, plus chilling time   Makes one 9" cheesecake

C heesecake is an ancient food that's evolved over time. According to AtlasObscura.com, a type of cheesecake was served at the first Olympus Games in 776 BC. Now, it seems every country has their version. In the US, New York style cheesecake uses heavy cream or sour cream. Chicago-style is lighter.

Ingredients for the Crust

2½ cups graham cracker crumbs

½ cup walnuts, finely chopped

¼ cup packed brown sugar

2 teaspoons ground cinnamon

¼ cup unsalted butter, melted

Ingredients for the Filling

24 ounces cream cheese, room temperature

2 cups sour cream, room temperature

1 cup granulated sugar

pinch of salt

1 teaspoon vanilla extract

3 large eggs, beaten

Making the Crust

1   Preheat oven to 350°.
2   Combine graham crackers, walnuts, brown sugar, cinnamon, and butter, and press into a 9" x 3" springform pan. Bring the sides of the crust all the way to the top edge of the pan. (Some people only create a base and not the sides—your choice.)
3   Bake for 10 to 15 minutes. Be sure not to overcook; if you do, the crust gets too hard. It'll cook more as you bake it with the filling.
4   Remove from oven and cool while making the filling.

Making the Filling and Finishing the Cheesecake

1   Cream the cream cheese really well, so it isn't lumpy.
2   Add sour cream and blend well.
3   Add sugar, salt, vanilla, and eggs and blend well.
4   Pour into the cooled crust and bake for about 1 hour or until a knife inserted halfway between the edge and the middle comes out clean.
5   Cool overnight in the refrigerator.

Perfect Pie Crust

Prep/cook time: 10 minutes   Makes two 9" pie crusts

Everyone's definition of perfect pie crust is going to be a little different. Mine is a pie crust that is tender and delicious without using lard or shortening. It took me many tries to develop a pie crust recipe that met my tastes. Here it is. To make this into a savory crust, replace the sugar and pinch of salt with 1 teaspoon salt. This recipe halves well.

2 cups all-purpose flour
2 teaspoons sugar
1 pinch salt

10 tablespoons unsalted butter, cold
2 tablespoons avocado oil
6 tablespoons ice-cold water

1   Combine the flour, sugar, and pinch of salt.
2   Cut in the butter and oil until the dough is the consistency of cornmeal.
3   One tablespoon at a time, sprinkle ice water on the flour mixture, blending gently with a fork.
4   Keep adding the water a tablespoon at a time until the mixture can be carefully and gently gathered with your hands into a ball. The dough should be silky and not wet.
5   Divide the dough into two equal balls, then roll out with a well-floured rolling pin on a well-floured board.
6   After putting the crust in a pie pan, place the pan in the refrigerator for about 30 minutes so the dough can relax. (This is the secret to not having your pie crust shrink quite so much when it bakes.)

Pumpkin Pie

Prep/cook time: 1 hour   Makes one 9″ pie

A tradition at American winter holiday dinners. Mix each set of ingredients well before adding the next set of ingredients. Because we love spices, this pie has more spices than most pumpkin pie recipes.

1 9-inch pie crust, unbaked	**½** teaspoon ground mace
15 ounces pumpkin purée	**½** teaspoon ground nutmeg
¼ teaspoon ground allspice	**¾** cup packed brown sugar
1 teaspoon ground cinnamon	**1** cup heavy cream
½ teaspoon ground cloves	**½** cup whole milk
½ teaspoon ground ginger	**2** large eggs, lightly beaten

1   Preheat oven to 375°.
2   Put pie crust in a 9" pan.
3   Combine pumpkin purée and spices. Mix well.
4   Add brown sugar to the pumpkin mix. Mix well.
5   Add cream and milk. Mix well.
6   Add eggs. Mix well.
7   Open oven and pull out a rack in the middle.
8   Place the pie pan with crust on the rack.
9   Carefully pour the pumpkin mixture into the pie crust. (This is to avoid spilling the filling.)
10 Carefully slide the rack into the oven and close the oven door.
11 Bake for 45 to 50 minutes or until the pie tests done. To test for doneness, insert a clean knife about 1 or 2 inches from the center. If it comes out clean, it's done.

Ritz Cracker Pie

Prep/cook time: 2 hours   Makes one 8" pie

The ingredients in this recipe sound improbable, but the pie, also known as Mock Apple Pie, is truly delicious. A co-worker in the 1980s often brought this pie to pot lucks and it was always completed devoured. I had to coax the recipe out of her, not because she didn't want to share it, but because she was afraid I wouldn't eat the pie anymore if I knew what was in it. *Au contraire.* You can make the pie the night before you plan to serve it, or you can freeze it now and serve it later. However, the pie gets soggy if the whipped cream is left on too long, so if you plan to freeze the pie and serve it later, freeze it without the whipped cream, then thaw and add the whipped cream right before serving. Instead of Ritz crackers, you can use Trader Joe's Golden Rounds.

3 large egg whites	**1** cup pecans or walnuts
1/4 teaspoon cream of tartar	**22** Ritz crackers, crushed
1 cup granulated sugar	**1** cup heavy cream
1/2 teaspoon baking powder	**3** tablespoons powdered sugar
1/2 teaspoon vanilla extract	**1/2** teaspoon vanilla

1   Grease an 8" pie pan.
2   Beat egg whites with cream of tartar until they stand in stiff peaks.
3   Gradually add sugar and baking powder.
4   Add vanilla.
5   Fold in nuts and crushed crackers.
6   Bake in greased pie pan at 350° for 30 minutes.
7   Remove from oven and cool the pie completely.
8   Whip the cream with the powdered sugar and vanilla.
9   Cover the top of the pie completely with whipped cream.

Sweet Quick Breads

Quick breads are savory or sweet breads that rise because of leavening (usually baking soda or baking powder) rather than yeast. Some examples of quick breads are banana bread, (American) biscuits, muffins (savory and sweet), and scones (savory and sweet). Technically, brownies and cakes are also quick breads, but in the US, we normally think of brownies as a form of bar cookie (see *Cookies* on page 63), and we think of cakes as, well, cake (see *Cakes and Cupcakes* on page 13).

One interesting cultural note: in one of my cooking forums, a Scottish person commented on how horrible American scones are. Turns out she had been eating American biscuits, which are neither what the UK would call a biscuit, nor are they scones (though they look scone-like, and the methods are similar). Instead, I hastened to assure her, American biscuits are things in themselves: small, savory quick breads with a specific texture and type of flavor. Since they're savory, you won't find biscuit recipes in this cookbook, though in the companion volume for this book, you'll find a never-fail, high-rising biscuit recipe that violates all the rules about handling biscuits gently.

Another interesting cultural note: for some reason, many Americans think that *all* quick breads must be sweet, so in the US, you'll find classic savory quick breads, such as Irish Soda Bread, sweetened and often sprinkled with sugar or even iced. I have opinions about this cultural trend.

In this chapter, I've included sweet quick breads only, not savory ones. These recipes are all especially great with tea. Interesting fact: about 50% of all Americans prefer tea over coffee. This surprises me. I assumed "everyone" drank coffee, and that I was the odd woman out. But nay nay, as the late, beloved John Pinette would say, and really, the American grocery store aisles and websites devoted to tea should have been a clue.

Coffee-lovers, these recipes are all perfectly delicious with coffee, too.

Almond Scones

Prep/cook time: 30 minutes   Makes 8 large scones

My daughter took a basic scone recipe and modified it so heavily that I consider this her recipe. This recipe produces a delicate, tender, irresistible scone studded with marzipan and chocolate chips—perfect for tea. It requires the lightest of touches; scones can't take much handling. I highly recommend making your own marzipan (see page 56)—it's so easy and much less expensive than buying it.

2 cups all-purpose flour
1/4 cup granulated sugar
1/2 tablespoon baking powder
1/2 teaspoon salt
1/2 tablespoon ground
   cinnamon

1/2 cup unsalted butter
5 ounces marzipan
1 1/4 cups heavy cream
1 teaspoon almond extract
1 cup semisweet chocolate
   chips

1   Combine dry ingredients.
2   Cut butter into the dry ingredients.
3   Cut the almond paste into the butter mixture until the almond paste is in half-inch pieces.
4   Add the cream and chocolate chips and combine very lightly. Even if the flour and the cream aren't completely mixed, don't overwork the dough.
5   Lightly flour a clean surface and place the dough on it.
6   Now, *very* gently fold the dough, then, again *very* gently, form the dough into a flattened circle about 1½ inches thick.
7   Cut the dough into pie-shaped wedges (or cut with a 3-inch biscuit cutter) and place on a lined baking sheet (silicone mats work well).
8   Let the scones rest for 10 minutes. Resting is one of the secrets to tender scones that rise well.
9   Bake at 350° for 15 to 20 minutes, or until the wedges are lightly golden.
10 Remove from oven and cool on wire racks.

Banana Muffins

Prep/cook time: 15 minutes   Makes 1 dozen muffins

This amazing gluten-free recipe is almost magical in how it produces delicious, fluffy muffins; even more impressive is that each muffin has almost 5 grams of protein. The recipe only takes five minutes to prepare. If you leave out the chocolate chips and use almond or cashew butter, it's a paleo recipe. (The only one in this book. By their very nature, most regular desserts are not paleo.) Many thanks to WholeLifestyleNutrition.com for the original version of this recipe. For the ingredients, use pure maple syrup, not pancake syrup, and use natural nut butter. By "natural," I mean a nut butter that only contains nuts and salt (peanut butter made only with peanuts and salt, almond butter made only with almonds and salt, cashew butter made only with cashews and salt—you get the picture). Don't use the no-stir "natural" nut butters—those use palm oil. The recipe will fail if you use a nut butter with additives.

2 medium bananas, mashed
2 large eggs, lightly beaten
2 tablespoons maple syrup
1 cup nut butter (almond, peanut, or cashew)

½ teaspoon baking soda
1 teaspoon vanilla extract
1 teaspoon apple cider vinegar
1½ cups chocolate chips

1   Preheat oven to 400°.
2   Prepare a standard muffin tin by greasing the cups very well with coconut oil, or by lining with cupcake liners. If you don't grease well or use liners, you'll have a hard time removing the muffins.
3   Combine the bananas, eggs, maple syrup, nut butter, baking soda, vanilla, and vinegar and mix very well.
4   Stir in the chocolate chips.
5   Fill muffin tin cups about ¾ full.
6   Bake for ten minutes or until a knife inserted in a muffin comes out clean (except for melted chocolate chips).
7   Remove from oven. Immediately remove from muffin tin and cool.

Cinnamon Loaf

Prep/cook time: 1 hour   Makes three 5½" x 3" loaves

These fantastic loaves smell fragrantly of cinnamon and have a tender, moist crumb and wonderful flavor. This recipe is lovely baked in a tea loaf pan.

½ cup unsalted butter, melted
4 large eggs, beaten
2 cups whole milk
1 teaspoon almond extract
4 cups all-purpose flour

2 cups plus 2 tablespoons granulated sugar
2 tablespoons baking powder
1 teaspoon ground nutmeg
5 teaspoons plus 2 teaspoons ground cinnamon
1 teaspoon salt

1   Lightly grease three mini loaf pans (5½" x 3") or one 9" x 5" loaf pan.
2   Pour melted butter into a medium mixing bowl. Beat in eggs, milk, and almond extract.
3   In a separate bowl, combine flour, the 2 cups sugar, baking powder, nutmeg, the 5 teaspoons cinnamon, and salt. Mix well.
4   Add egg mixture to the flour mixture and stir lightly until just mixed.
5   Pour into prepared loaf pans.
6   Combine the 2 tablespoons sugar with the 2 teaspoons cinnamon and evenly sprinkle over each loaf.
7   Bake at 350° about 30 minutes. If baking in a larger loaf pan, bake a little longer.
8   Remove from oven and cool ten minutes, then remove from pans and cool on wire racks.

Fruitcake

Prep/cook time: 2 to 3 hours   Makes four 8" x 4" loaves

Like many people, I thought I didn't like fruitcake; mostly because of the candied fruit and citron. I changed my mind when I learned you could use delicious dried fruits instead. Some dried fruits that taste especially good in this recipe are apples, apricots, blueberries, cherries, currants, peaches, pears, unsweetened pineapple, and raisins. Along with the nuts, you could also use some flaked or shredded coconut. This recipe uses whole wheat pastry flour, which holds up well to the fruit and adds a delicately heartier flavor. You'll need three bowls to make this bread.

8 cups mixed pitted, dried fruit
2 cups coarsely chopped nuts
    (pecans, walnuts, or a mix)
2½ cups whole wheat pastry
    flour
1 teaspoon baking powder
1 teaspoon salt
1½ teaspoons ground
    cinnamon

1 teaspoon ground nutmeg
1 teaspoon ground cloves
½ teaspoon ground allspice
½ cup unsalted butter,
    softened
½ cup honey
4 large eggs
1 tablespoon molasses
¼ cup brandy

1   Prepare four 8" x 4" loaf pans by lining with parchment paper or greasing well.
2   **Bowl 1**: In a large bowl, combine the dried fruit and nuts with a few tablespoons of the flour, coating the pieces well.
3   **Bowl 2**: In a separate bowl, combine the remainder of the flour, baking powder, salt, and spices.
4   **Bowl 3**: In a third large bowl, cream the butter, honey, eggs, and molasses, then stir in the brandy when the other ingredients are creamy and well mixed.
5   Stir the flour mixture of **Bowl 2** into the butter mixture in **Bowl 3**.
6   Gently fold in the fruits and nuts (**Bowl 1**) into **Bowl 3**.
7   Spoon the batter into prepared loaf pans.
8   Bake at 325° for 1 to 1½ hours, or until a knife inserted in the center comes out clean.
9   Remove from oven and cool ten minutes, then remove from pans and cool on wire racks.
10 Pour some brandy over the loaves. Wrap in cheesecloth and store in a cool place. Periodically renew the brandy.

Nut Bread

Prep/cook time: 1 hour 15 minutes   Makes two 9" x 5" loaves

This unusual quick nut bread is light and uniquely tasty. Walnuts and pecans are great in this recipe.

4 cups all-purpose flour
1 tablespoon salt
2 tablespoon baking powder
2 teaspoons ground cinnamon
1½ cups chopped nuts

2 large eggs
1¼ cups granulated sugar
2 cups whole milk
¼ cup unsalted butter, melted

1   Lightly grease two 9" x 5" loaf pans.
2   In a large bowl, mix the flour, salt, baking powder, and cinnamon together.
3   Add the remaining ingredients in order, mixing well after each addition.
4   Pour into prepared loaf pans. Bake at 350° for 1 hour or until done.
5   Remove from oven and cool ten minutes, then remove from pans and cool on wire racks.

Orange Tea Bread

Prep/cook time: 1½ hours   Makes one 9" x 5" loaf

This bread is a trifle syrupy in a thoroughly delicious way. It's perfect with tea. You can replace the orange juice, orange zest, and sugar mixture with 1 cup orange marmalade (thinned with water) and ½ cup sugar.

1 cup orange juice	**2** cups all-purpose flour
zest of two oranges	**1** cup oat flour
1½ cups granulated sugar	**¼** teaspoon salt
1 large egg, lightly beaten	**1** tablespoon baking powder
1 cup whole milk	

1   Grease a 9" x 5" loaf pan.
2   Simmer the orange juice and zest in a medium saucepan for 5 minutes.
3   Add the sugar and boil to a syrup until it threads slightly (230° to 234°).
4   Remove syrup from heat and cool for ten minutes.
5   In a small bowl, beat the eggs and milk together.
6   Add the eggs/milk mixture to the cooled syrup.
7   In a medium bowl, combine the flours, salt, and baking powder.
8   Add the flour mixture to the syrup mixture.
9   Pour batter into prepared loaf pan. Bake at 350° for 50 minutes or until done.
10 Remove from oven and cool ten minutes, then remove from pans and cool on wire racks.

Persimmon Bread

Prep/cook time: 2 hours   Makes one 10" Bundt bread

When I first got this recipe, it was called Persimmon Pudding, using the British definition of pudding as a general name for dessert. That proved to be too confusing for people, because it's really a moist, dense, heavy bread. After much happy experimentation with various quantities and ingredients, I've come up with something that even those who dislike persimmons love. It keeps well, so it makes an excellent gift bread. I use Hachiya persimmons plucked from my tree and ripened until the pulp is a lovely, deep red-orange and is soft and semi-translucent. You can use a single type of dried fruit, or any combination of currants, golden or regular raisins, dried cherries, dried cranberries, dried strawberries, and dried blueberries. Serve warm or cool with Hard Sauce (page 115).

2 cups granulated sugar
2 cups all-purpose flour
1½ teaspoons baking soda
1½ teaspoons baking powder
½ teaspoon salt
2 teaspoons ground cinnamon

2 large eggs, well beaten
2 cups ripe persimmon pulp
2 cups walnuts, chopped
2 cups small dried fruits
1 cup whole milk
¼ cup unsalted butter, melted

1   Grease two 9" loaf pans or one 12-cup Bundt pan.
2   Mix the dry ingredients together in a 4-quart mixing bowl.
3   Mix the eggs, persimmon, walnuts, dried fruits, milk, and butter in a 2-quart mixing bowl.
4   Combine the wet mixture with the dry mixture. Stir well.
5   Pour into prepared pans.
6   Bake at 325° for 1½ hours or until done. (A cake tester should come out clean.)
7   Remove from oven and cool ten minutes, then remove from pans and cool on a wire rack.

Shortcakes

Prep/cook time: 30 minutes   Makes about 6 shortcakes

A shortcake is a slightly sweetened quick bread that's often used as part of a dessert, such as strawberry shortcake. Most shortcake recipes use either a biscuit-type dough or a scone-type dough. This recipe, adapted from Stephanie Jaworski's JoyofBaking.com, is a cross between both types. Although this recipe calls for cream, you can use half-and-half, milk, or buttermilk; however, you'll get the richest flavor with cream. Serve with jam and clotted cream or butter, or cut in half, top each half with a fruit compote, then top with plenty of whipped cream.

2 cups all-purpose flour
1/4 cup granulated sugar
2 teaspoons baking powder
1/4 teaspoon kosher salt

1/3 cup unsalted butter
1 large egg, beaten lightly
1 teaspoon vanilla extract
1/2 cup heavy cream

1 Preheat oven to 375° and line a large baking sheet with parchment paper or a silicone baking liner (not aluminum—the shortcakes will burn).
2 Combine the flour, sugar, baking powder, and salt.
3 Cut the butter into the flour mixture until the mixture looks like coarse meal.
4 In a separate bowl, combine the egg, vanilla, and cream.
5 Add the egg mixture to the flour mixture, mixing just until the dough forms and all the flour is moistened. As with most biscuit- and scone-style quick breads, you want to handle the dough as little as possible to keep it tender.
6 Gather the dough and place on a floured surface. Knead gently a few times, then roll out to a thickness of 3/4 inch. Cut out shortcakes with a 3-inch round cookie cutter. Place on the prepared baking sheet, spacing about 1 inch apart. Gently gather the scraps and roll out again. At the end, shape one more shortcake by hand for a charmingly rough look.
7 Bake 15 to 20 minutes or until the shortcakes are a lovely golden brown on top. Test for doneness with a cake tester. When the tester comes out clean, the shortcakes are done.
8 Remove from oven and from the baking sheet. Cool the shortcakes on a wire rack.

Weights and Measures

For those of you cooking in other units, this chapter has many common weight and volume equivalents (including metric). You'll also find all the tables from earlier in the book, including an expanded version of the baking pan size table from the *Cakes and Cupcakes* chapter. And you'll find a table of sugar terms in the US and United Kingdom (UK).

The tables in this chapter are not exhaustive. To convert other quantities than in the tables in this chapter, I highly recommend the following pages:

- For almost every possible conversion, I relied heavily on this site to create the list of equivalent weights: convert-me.com/en/convert/cooking/. (That site has been on the Internet since 1995!)
- For a list of all kinds of flours in cups, ounces, and grams, see kingarthurflour.com/learn/ingredient-weight-chart.html
- For lists of ingredients in US measurements and their UK equivalents, see allrecipes.co.uk/how-to/44/cooking-conversions.aspx
- For different types of converters for several specific cooking ingredients, see traditionaloven.com/tutorials/conversion.html

As with everything else in this book, the tables in this chapter are in alphabetical order. In the tables of weights and measures, I've rounded to the nearest whole number in most cases. Exact precision isn't essential in any of these recipes.

Baking Pan Sizes

In the *Cakes and Cupcakes* chapter (which starts on page 13), I include an abbreviated version of the following table of baking pan sizes and capacities. **Note that baking pan sizes can vary.** One mini loaf pan may be a different size than another. To do your own conversions, 1 inch = 2.54 centimeters; 1 cup = 237 milliliters (ml). Measure pans from the inside, not the outside.

Baking pans by size and volume (long table)

Size in inches	Approximate size in centimeters	Approximate capacity in US cups	Approximate capacity in liters or milliliters
Bundt and tube pans			
4 x 1¾ Bundt mini	10 x 4.5	1	237 ml
4½ x 2 tube mini	11.5 x 5	1¼	296 ml
7½ x 3 Bundt	19 x 8	6	1.4 liters
9 x 3 Bundt or tube	23 x 8	12	2.8 liters
10 x 4 Bundt or tube	25 x 10	16	3.8 liters
Heart-shaped pans			
8 x 2½	20 x 6	8	1.9 liters
Jelly roll pans			
15½ x 10½ x 1	39 x 27 x 2.5	10	2.4 liters
17½ x 12½ x 1	44 x 32 x 2.5	12	2.8 liters
Loaf pans			
5½ x 3 x 2½ (mini)	14 x 7 x 6	2⅔	633 ml
7⅜ x 3⅝ x 2	20 x 8.6 x 5	3	711 ml
8 x 4 x 2½	20 x 10 x 6	4	948 ml
8½ x 4½ x 2½	21 x 11 x 6	6	1.4 liters
9 x 5 x 3	23 x 13 x 8	8	1.9 liters
12 x 4 x 2½ (tea loaf)	30 x 10 x 6	8	1.9 liters
Muffin tins			
1¾ x ¾ (mini)	4.5 x 2	⅛ (per well)	30 ml
2¾ x 1½ (standard)	7 x 4	½ (per well)	118 ml
3¼ x 1¼ (jumbo)	8 x 3	⅞ (per well)	150 ml

Size in inches	Approximate size in centimeters	Approximate capacity in US cups	Approximate capacity in liters or milliliters
Pie pans			
8 x 1¼	20 x 3	3	711 ml
9 x 2	23 x 5	6	1.4 liters
9½ x 2 (deep dish)	24 x 5	7	1.7 liters
10 x 1½	25 x 4	6	1.4 liters
Rectangular pans			
8 x 8	20 x 20	6	1.4 liters
9 x 9	23 x 23	8	1.9 liters
11 x 7 x 2	28 x 18 x 5	8	1.9 liters
13 x 9 x 2	33 x 29 x 5	14	3.3 liters
Round pans (cake and springform)			
6 x 2 cake	15 x 5	4	948 ml
6 x 3 springform	15 x 8	4	948 ml
7 x 2½ springform	18 x 6	5½	1.3 liters
8 x 1½ cake	20 x 4	4	948 ml
8 x 2 cake or springform	20 x 5	6	1.4 liters
8 x 3 springform	20 x 8	10	2.4 liters
9 x 1½ cake	23 x 4	6	1.4 liters
9 x 1¾ cake	23 x 4.5	7½	1.8 liters
9 x 2 cake	23 x 5	8	1.9 liters
9 x 2½ springform	23 X 6	10	2.4 liters
9 x 3 cake	23 x 8	12	2.8 liters
9 x 3 springform	23 x 8	12	2.8 liters
10 x 2 cake	25 x 5	11	2.6 liters
10 x 2½ springform	25 x 6	12	2.8 liters
12 x 2 cake	30.5 x 5	15	3.5 liters
14 x 2 cake	35.5 x 5	21	5 liters
Square pans			
8 x 8 x 2	20 x 20 x 5	8	1.9 liters
9 x 9 x 2	23 x 23 x 5	10	2.4 liters
10 x 10 x 2	25 x 25 x 5	12	2.8 liters

Egg Sizes and Substitutions

Unless otherwise specified, eggs in these recipes are large, US Grade AA or A chicken eggs. You can substitute small, medium, extra large, or jumbo chicken eggs, but you may need to adjust how many eggs you use.

Goose eggs, which are much larger than chicken eggs, are often used in European baking, so I've included the equivalents for goose eggs. If you need to divide a goose egg, beat the egg first.

Egg size substitutions table

If the recipe calls for this many chicken eggs	Use this many chicken eggs				Or this many goose eggs
Large eggs	Jumbo	Extra large	Medium	Small	(144 grams per egg)
1	1	1	1	1	½
2	2	2	2	3	1
3	2	3	3	4	1½
4	3	4	5	5	2
5	4	4	6	7	2½
6	5	5	7	8	3

In addition to goose eggs, you can also use duck, ostrich, or even quail. Here are the average weights for those eggs, plus a few notes.

- **Duck eggs** weigh about 70 grams, about the same as a jumbo chicken egg in the US. Use the "Jumbo" column in the egg size substitutions table for how many duck eggs to use. Duck egg shells are thicker than chicken eggs (so they're harder to crack) and, depending on what the duck eats, the flavor can be stronger.
- **Ostrich eggs** weigh 3.5 to 5 pounds (1,600 to 2,300 grams), and are about the equivalent of 28 to 41 large US chicken eggs. With eggs that big, it doesn't make sense to talk about substituting numbers of eggs. Instead, beat the ostrich egg and weigh out how much you need. For example, if you're replacing 2 large chicken eggs, you'll need 142 grams of ostrich egg.
- **Quail eggs** weigh about 9 grams. You need about six quail eggs to substitute for one large chicken egg in the US.

The following table shows the standard chicken egg size names and weights in grams for Australia (AU), Canada (CA), the Europe Union (EU), New Zealand

(NZ), and the US. The data were taken from the websites of each country's equivalent of the United States Department of Agriculture (USDA).

Standard chicken egg weights in grams in different countries

Chicken egg size	AU	CA	EU	NZ	US
King size (AU)	73 g				
Mega, XXXL (Western AU)	72 g				
Jumbo	68 g	70 g		68 g	70.9 g
Extra large (XL)	60 g	63 g	73 g	62 g	63.8 g
Large (L; NZ: standard)	52 g	56 g	63 g	53 g	56.7 g
Medium (M)	43 g	49 g	53 g	44 g	49.6 g
Small (S)		42 g	>53 g		42.5 g
Peewee (NZ: pullet)		>42 g		35 g	35.4 g

Freezing Eggs

You'll often find you have leftover egg whites or yolks. You can freeze raw eggs, either the whole egg (never in the shell), or just the yolks or whites. Freeze eggs in labeled freezer-safe containers. Eggs can keep in the freezer for up to a year.

- For whole eggs, beat lightly before packaging, labeling, and freezing.
- For yolks, mix with ⅛ teaspoon salt (or 1½ teaspoons sugar) per ¼ cup of yolks (¼ cup is about four yolks). The salt (or sugar) helps slow down the yolk becoming gelatinous. Then package, label, and freeze.
- For whites, package, label, and freeze.

When labeling, include the number of eggs (or yolks or whites), whether you used salt or sugar, and the date. To use frozen yolks or whole eggs, thaw overnight in the refrigerator, then use immediately. If using thawed whites, bring to room temperature, then use immediately.

Eggnog lovers, you can freeze commercial eggnog (but not homemade—never freeze that) for up to six months.

For more on eggs, including nutrition, safe handling, and what you can and can't freeze. see the USDA's "Shell Eggs from Farm to Table" (fsis.usda.gov/wps/portal/fsis/topics/food-safety-education/get-answers/food-safety-fact-sheets/egg-products-preparation/shell-eggs-from-farm-to-table/#17).

Ingredient Weights and Measures

Imagine that you have one cup of feathers and one cup of rocks. They are both one cup in volume, but the rocks weigh much more. Likewise, the same *volume* of different food ingredients can *weigh* differently. For example, one cup of powdered sugar weighs less than one cup of granulated sugar. Because many cooks use weights rather than volumes, and many US recipes specify volume (including this book), it's useful to know how much something weighs.

In addition, measuring cups and spoons vary from country to country. For example, measuring cups and spoons in the UK are slightly larger than in the US; 1 UK cup holds a bit more than 1 US cup. And fluid ounces are also different between the US and the UK (because the ounces are from different systems).

With ingredients you use in smaller quantities, the volume difference isn't important: 1 teaspoon of vanilla extract (which is called vanilla essence in the UK and Australia) is going to be fine whether it's a US teaspoon or a UK teaspoon. (The exception is salt—small variations in salt are quite noticeable.) But with the ingredients you use in larger quantities, the difference can be important.

For the common ingredients used in this book where weight or volume can make a difference (butter, sugar, flour, and so on), the following table lists those ingredients with their weights and volumes in US, UK, and metric units. (I've rounded most UK and metric units.) You'll need to do a little math to figure out the units not listed in this table. For example, if a recipe calls for ½ cup sugar, divide the US 1 cup weight and volume for sugar in half. For other volumes or weights, see the conversion websites listed on page 149.

If you live in the UK and you don't want to fuss with conversions, US measuring cups and spoons are available to buy online in the UK.

Weights and volumes for specific ingredients

Ingredient	US Units	UK Units	Metric Units
Butter	2 cups (16 ounces)	2 cups	454 grams
Butter	1 cup (8 ounces)	1 cup	227 grams
Butter	½ cup (4 ounces)	½ cup	114 grams
Buttermilk, sour cream, yogurt	½ cup (4 fluid ounces)	.46 cup (4.2 fluid ounces)	118 ml
Buttermilk, sour cream, yogurt	⅓ cup (2.6 fluid ounces)	.32 cup (2.7 fluid ounces)	78.8 ml
Chocolate chips	1 cup (6 ounces)	.95 cup	170 grams
Cocoa powder	1 cup (3.5 ounces)	.9 cup	100 grams
Cream, heavy (double cream)	1 cup (8 fluid ounces)	.98 cup (8.3 fluid ounces)	237 ml

Ingredient	US Units	UK Units	Metric Units
Flour, all purpose, unsifted (plain flour)	1 cup (4.25 ounces)	.96 cup	120 grams
Flour, almond (almond meal)	1 cup (3.4 ounces)	1 cup	96 grams
Milk, whole	1 cup (8 fluid ounces)	.98 cup (8.3 fluid ounces)	237 ml
Sugar, brown	1 cup (7 ounces)	.9 cup	198 grams
Sugar, granulated	1 cup (7.1 ounces)	.9 cup	200 grams
Sugar, powdered (icing sugar)	1 cup (4.4 ounces)	.9 cup	125 grams
Sugar, superfine (castor sugar)	1 cup (7.9 ounces)	.9 cup	225 grams

Remember that the fluid ounce systems in the US and UK are different. And note that these are all as close as I could get, but volumes and weights can vary.

Oven Temperatures and Formulas

Different countries use different temperature systems. For guidelines on oven temperatures, see page 9. For your convenience, I've repeated the table of oven temperatures from that section.

Note that the Celsius temperatures in this table are the conventional equivalents, not the precise equivalents. in baking, a precise temperature isn't usually vital as long as you're close enough.

If you want a precise equivalent, you'll need to do a tiny bit of math: to convert from Fahrenheit to Celsius, take the temperature in degrees Fahrenheit (°F), subtract 32, then multiply the result by $\frac{5}{9}$ (which is .5555). The final number is the temperature in degrees Celsius (°C). Here's the formula:

```
((Temperature in °F) - 32) × .5555 = temperature in °C
```

So, for example, to convert 350°F to its Celsius equivalent,

```
(350°F - 32) x .5555 = 176.6649°C or 177°C, rounded
```

The formula to go the other way (from degrees Celsius to degrees Fahrenheit) is as follows:

```
(Temperature in °C x 1.8) + 32 = temperature in °F
```

Oven temperature equivalents

Fahrenheit (°F)	Celsius (°C)	Gas Mark	Descriptive Term
150 to 194	66 to 90	NA	Drying
200 to 230	93 to 110	1/4	Very slow/very low
248 to 266	120 to 130	1/2 or .5	Very slow/very low
275	140	1	Slow/low
300	150	2	Slow/low
325	160	3	Moderately slow/warm
350	180	4	Moderate/medium
375	190	5	Moderate/moderately hot
400	200	6	Moderately hot
425	210	7	Hot
450	220	8	Hot/very hot
475	240	9	Very hot
500	260	10	Extremely hot

Sugar Terms and Stages

The following table pairs the US term for different types of sugar with the UK terms. For a description of the different types of sugar, see Types of Sugars on page 5.

Sugar types and terms

US Term	UK Term
Brown sugar, light	Demerara sugar
Brown sugar, dark	Dark soft sugar
Granulated sugar, white sugar, sugar	Baking sugar, sugar
Molasses	Black treacle
Powdered sugar, confectioner's sugar	Frosting sugar, icing sugar
Superfine sugar, baker's sugar	Castor (or caster) sugar

The following table summarizes the sugar stages in candy cooking. For details on these stages, see Sugar Stages (page 45).

Sugar stages and temperatures

Stage	Example	Fahrenheit (°F)	Celsius (°C)
Thread	Syrup	230 to 234	110 to 112
Soft ball	Fudge, fondant	235 to 241	112 to 116
Firm ball	Caramel	244 to 248	118 to 120
Hard ball	Taffy	250 to 266	121 to 130
Soft crack	Saltwater taffy	270 to 289	132 to 143
Hard crack	Nut brittles	295 to 309	146 to 154
Clear liquid	NA	320	160
Brown liquid	Caramelized sugar	338	170
Burnt sugar	Burnt sugar	350	177

Index